# FURTHER *Curriculum Bank*

# SCIENCE

## KEY STAGE ONE / SCOTTISH LEVELS A–B

**GEORGIE BEASLEY AND BRIAN PENGELLY**

**Published by Scholastic Ltd,**
Villiers House,
Clarendon Avenue,
Leamington Spa,
Warwickshire CV32 5PR
Text © Georgie Beasley and Brian Pengelly
© 1999  Scholastic Ltd
1 2 3 4 5 6 7 8 9 0   9 0 1 2 3 4 5 6 7 8

Authors
**Georgie Beasley and Brian Pengelly**

Editor
**Kate Pearce**

Assistant editor
**Clare Miller**

Series designer
**Rachel Warner**

Designer
**Sarah Rock**

Illustrations
**Kirsty Wilson**

Cover illustration
**Lesley Saddington**

Scottish 5–14 links
**Margaret Scott and Susan Gow**

**Acknowledgements**
© **Crown copyright 1995**. Material from the National
Curriculum, Scottish 5–14 Guidelines and the Northern
Ireland Curriculum is reproduced by permission of the
Controller of Her Majesty's Stationery Office.
**A.C. Cooper** for photographs of the front cover illustrations
© 1999, A.C. Cooper

British Library Cataloguing-in-Publication Data
A catalogue record for this book is available from
the British Library.

ISBN 0-590-53875-6

The right of Georgie Beasley and Brian Pengelly to be
identified as the Authors of this Work has been asserted
by them in accordance with the Copyright, Designs and
Patents Act 1988.

# Contents

# Introduction

Welcome to *Further Curriculum Bank Science* (Key Stage One/Scottish Levels A–B). This book provides a bank of practical science activities. The bank of activities can easily be incorporated into any scheme of work. It also complements those contained in the original book *Curriculum Bank Science*.

This book is divided into three sections: Life Processes and Living Things (Sc2); Materials and their Properties (Sc3); and Physical Processes (Sc4). At the end of the book there is a bank of photocopiable sheets which can be used to support the practical science contained in the lesson plans or as a bank of ideas for you to adapt to suit your needs.

All the lessons in this book are relevant to the development of ideas contained in the introduction to the Science Programme of Study (Sc0). The lessons require children to undertake systematic enquiry, to communicate their ideas and provide evidence to justify their conclusions. Health and Safety issues are highlighted in the text with a safety symbol ▲. In addition to carrying out normal risk assessment procedures, we recommend that, whenever possible, teachers involve pupils in the process of risk assessment. In this way the children will learn how to minimise risks for themselves.

The philosophy behind the science activities in this book is that children should be actively involved in the development of their own science concepts and skills. Wherever possible, the lessons build on experiences that are part of everyday life: food, plants, clothing, the weather and other features of the natural and man-made world. All the lessons could form starting points for science work with young children but where prior knowledge would be helpful this is indicated in the text.

We believe that children need to develop an appropriate vocabulary to help them to develop and communicate their ideas and understanding. Language relevant to each activity is provided. It may be helpful to provide the new words on a sheet for adult helpers or as part of a display for children's reference.

Due to the practical nature of the activities we have relied on the availability of parent helpers and classroom assistants to increase the adult:pupil ratio for some lessons. You may find it useful to provide your helpers with two or three assessment questions. Ideas for assessment are included in the text. Alternatively, you might ask a helper to observe your teacher-led plenary session and to record some of the pupil responses for you.

All the lessons contain elements of Experimental and Investigative Science. With young children, there is a natural emphasis on the development of observational and sorting/classifying skills. The symbol ⊕ indicates that an activity contains a complete investigation. However, all the activities contained in this book offer opportunities to involve the children in the planning of experimental work and in the collection and analysis of evidence. The development of these high order skills will help your pupils become better investigative scientists and give them a scientific lens through which to view their world.

We hope that you enjoy using these activities.

**Lesson plans**
The structure for each activity is as follows:

*Activity title box*
The box at the beginning of each activity outlines the following key aspects:
▲ *Learning objective.* The learning objectives break down aspects of the Programme of Study for science into manageable teaching and learning chunks. They can easily be referenced to the National Curriculum for England and Wales and the Scottish National Guidelines 5–14 by using the overview grid on pages 7–11.
▲ *Class organization/Likely duration.* The icons ✝✝ and 🕐 indicate the suggested group sizes for each activity and the approximate amount of time required to complete it.

*Previous skills/knowledge needed*
This section gives information when it is necessary for the children to have acquired specific knowledge or skills prior to carrying out the activity.

*Key background information*
This section outlines the areas of study covered by the activity and gives a general background to the topic or theme, outlining the basic skills that will be developed and the way in which the activity will address the children's learning.

*Preparation*
This section indicates when it is necessary for the teacher to prime the pupils for the activity, to prepare materials or to set up a display or activity prior to the lesson.

*Resources needed*
All materials needed to carry out the activity, including photocopiable pages from this book, are listed here.

*Vocabulary*
Scientific words essential to the activity are listed here. They can be displayed, referred to during discussion and used by the children when recording.

*What to do*
Clear step-by-step instructions are given for carrying out the activity, including (where appropriate) suitable questions for the teacher to ask the children in order to help instigate discussion and stimulate investigation.

*Suggestion(s) for extension/support*
In these sections, ways of providing differentiation are suggested.

*Assessment opportunities*
Where appropriate, opportunities for ongoing teacher assessment of the children's work during or after the activity are highlighted.

*Opportunities for IT*
Where relevant IT work would strengthen an activity, appropriate possibilities are outlined with reference to suitable types of program.

*Display ideas*
Where they are relevant and innovative, display ideas are incorporated into the activity plans and illustrated with examples.

*Reference to photocopiable sheets*
Photocopiable activity sheets are provided for use with particular activities. Small reproductions of these are included in the appropriate lesson plans, together with notes on their use and (where appropriate) suggested answers to questions.

# Overview Grid

This grid helps you to track the coverage of the Programme of Study for Science at Key Stage One, or the Scottish National Guidelines for Environmental Studies 5–14 at Levels C–E, offered by the activities in this book. For each activity, the relevant statements from the National Curriculum for England and Wales and the Scottish 5–14 Guidelines are indicated (the latter references are given in italics). Most of the activities in this book can be used alongside the activities in the Curriculum Bank for Science at Key Stage One/Scottish Levels A–B. These links are indicated by footnotes in the shaded panel below the relevant activities.

| ACTIVITY TITLE | LEARNING OBJECTIVE | POS/AO | CONTENT | PAGE |
|---|---|---|---|---|
| **Shoes** | We use our hands and fingers to find out by touching. | LP 2f *Processes of Life Level A* | Matching footwear by using our sense of touch. Whole class then individuals. | 12 |
| **Feely bags, page 15** | | | | |
| **Squidgy feelings!** | We use our sense of touch to find out some properties of foods. | LP 2f *As above* | Exploring feely bags of food using our sense of touch. Group activity. | 14 |
| **Feeling surfaces, page 14; Feely bags, page 15** | | | | |
| **Tickling toes** | We can use our feet for feeling. | LP 2f *As above* | Investigating the texture of different flooring samples using bare feet. Whole class then group activity. | 16 |
| **Feeling surfaces, page 14** | | | | |
| **Match my sound** | We use our sense of hearing to find out about the world. | LP 2f *As above* | Matching different sounds. Class introduction. Individual/paired activity. | 18 |
| **Exploring sound, page 18** | | | | |
| **Identifying Archie** | We use our eyes and sense of sight to notice detail and help us find out about things around us. | LP 2f *As above* | Identifying an object from a range of both different and similar objects. Class activity. | 20 |
| **Find my colour** | We use our sense of sight to find out about the world around us. | LP 2f *As above* | Matching colours to natural objects in the environment. Class introduction. Group activity. | 22 |
| **Seeing is believing, page 16** | | | | |
| **Coloured milk** | Our mouths and tongues give us a sense of taste which helps us to make decisions about flavours. | LP 2f *As above* | Predicting whether different-coloured milks will taste different. Completing a photocopiable record sheet. Individual within group activity. | 24 |
| **Taste, page 18** | | | | |
| **Who am I?** | Some things about us are different and some are the same. | LP 4a *As above* | A matching game based on descriptions of children in the class. | 26 |
| **What colour eyes?, page 30** | | | | |

**LIFE PROCESSES AND LIVING THINGS**

| ACTIVITY TITLE | LEARNING OBJECTIVE | POS/AO | CONTENT | PAGE |
|---|---|---|---|---|
| **Are these my hands?** | We all grow. | LP 1b *Taking Action on Health Level A* | Class activity. Exploring a range and variety of photocopied hands. Group activity within a class lesson. | 28 |
| **Babies, page 27; Growing children, page 29** | | | | |
| **Healthy food plates** | We eat different types of food, and eating the right types and amounts of food helps to keep us healthy. | LP 2c *As above* | Considering healthy and unhealthy food choices. Class then group activity. | 30 |
| **Health and happiness, page 24** | | | | |
| **Leaves** | Living things can be grouped according to similarities and differences. | LP 4b *Processes of Life Level A* | Sorting a collection of leaves by size, shape, colour, pattern and texture. Group activity. | 31 |
| **Sorting seeds, page 32; Knock --- on wood, page 48** | | | | |
| **Mung beans** | Plants need water and light to become fully grown. | LP 3a *As above* | Growing mung beans using different conditions and comparing the effect on their growth. Class or group activity. | 33 |
| **Plants need light and water, page 35** | | | | |
| **Pumpkins** | Seeds grow into plants and plants grow. | LP 3c *As above* | Growing pumpkin seeds and comparing the growth and features of the plants. Class or group activity. | 35 |
| **Planting seeds, page 33; Sunflower competition, page 37** | | | | |
| **One potato, two potatoes** | To make careful observations, notice change and record findings in an investigation about potatoes. | LP 3c *As above* | Investigating the effect on potatoes when they are stored in different places. Class or group activity. | 37 |
| **Minibeast safari** | Animals are all around us. | LP 5a *Variety and Characteristic Features Level B* | Identifying small creatures in the school grounds. Class activity. | 40 |
| **Animals at school, page 39** | | | | |
| **Birds** | Different species of the same animal sometimes visit the same habitat. | LP 5a *As above Level A* | Observing the types and species of birds that visit the school playground. Class observation activity. | 42 |
| **Birds, page 93** | | | | |
| **Wriggling worms** | Animals move, feed and grow. | LP1b *Variety and Characteristic Features Level B* | Observing worms in a wormery. Class activity. | 44 |
| **Snails, page 42** | | | | |

| | ACTIVITY TITLE | LEARNING OBJECTIVE | POS/AO | CONTENT | PAGE |
|---|---|---|---|---|---|
| **MATERIALS AND THEIR PROPERTIES** | **Soils** | We use our senses to recognize the properties of certain materials. | 1a<br>*Materials from Earth Level A* | Sorting and labelling a collection of soils using the senses of smell, touch and sight.<br>Class activity organized into groups of 4 or 6. | 47 |
| | **Pouring oil over water** | To explore materials and objects using appropriate senses, making observations and communicating these. | 1a<br>*As above* | Looking at different objects and predicting whether they will float or sink. Exploring and investigating what happens when oil is poured on water.<br>Class introduction followed by small group work. | 49 |
| | **Sort out your colour table** | To be able to sort objects into sets of common materials and to recognize some of the properties. | 1b<br>*As above* | Sorting a collection of materials according to their properties.<br>Class introduction followed by group activity. | 51 |
| | **I can see right through, page 50** | | | | |
| | **Rock in a sock** | We can use our sense of touch to explore a range of common materials and use our knowledge of properties to identify them. | 1c<br>*As above* | A game to identify paper, rock, metal, fabric, plastic and wood through touch.<br>Group activity. | 53 |
| | **Knock --- on wood, page 48; Naming materials, page 53** | | | | |
| | **A plastic world** | Different everyday objects can be made from materials we call plastics. | 1d<br>*Materials from Earth Level B* | An activity to explore and identify the different uses of plastic.<br>Class introduction followed by group investigation. | 55 |
| | **Feeling surfaces, page 14; Feely bags, page 15** | | | | |
| | **Don't burst my bubble!** | To learn that some materials have different uses and use this concept to develop the skills of investigation. | 1d<br>*As above* | Investigating a variety of bubble makers and bubble mixtures. Evaluating what makes a good bubble blower.<br>Class activity followed by group recording using a photocopiable sheet. | 57 |
| | **Materials with many uses, page 54** | | | | |
| | **Tie yourself in knots** | Materials are chosen for specific purposes based on their properties. | 1e<br>*As above* | Exploring a variety of materials to ascertain which ones make good laces.<br>Group activity. | 59 |
| | **Gloves to keep you warm** | Materials are chosen for specific purposes because of their properties. | 1e<br>*As above* | Investigating the different materials from which gloves are made. Testing different materials for their insulation properties.<br>Class introduction followed by group investigation. | 61 |
| | **Materials with special uses, page 55** | | | | |

| ACTIVITY TITLE | LEARNING OBJECTIVE | POS/AO | CONTENT | PAGE |
|---|---|---|---|---|
| **Bend your image** | Materials are chosen for specific purposes. Some materials and their purpose can be changed by bending. | 2a<br>*Materials from Earth Level B* | Investigating different types of mirrors including concave and convex mirrors. Looking at the different images they reflect. Class or group activity. | 64 |
| **Springy things** | Some materials and their characteristics can be changed by bending. | 2a<br>*As above* | Investigating different types of springs. Considering which everyday objects contain springs. Making springs from card and wire and using these to play a game. Group activity. | 66 |
| *The bendy puppet, page 59* | | | | |
| **Popcorn** | Many materials change when heated. | 2b<br>*As above* | Considering cooked and uncooked corn. Considering how some foods change when they are cooked. Making popcorn. Class or group activity. | 68 |
| **Burnt toast and hard cheese** | Materials change when heated. | 2b<br>*As above* | Considering how some foods change when they are heated Making toasted cheese and looking at the changes that have taken place in the foodstuffs used. Class activity. | 70 |
| *Melting chocolate, page 65* | | | | |

**PHYSICAL PROCESSES**

| ACTIVITY TITLE | LEARNING OBJECTIVE | POS/AO | CONTENT | PAGE |
|---|---|---|---|---|
| **Batteries must be included!** | An electrical device will not work if there is a break in the circuit. | 1c<br>*Forms and Sources of Energy Level B* | Exploring a collection of torches and the circuits needed for them to work. Group activity. | 73 |
| *Electricity and safety, page 68; Using electricity, page 69; Making simple circuits, page 71; Switching on and off, page 72* | | | | |
| **Push and pull** | To identify pushes and pulls and understand that pushes and pulls are forces which make things start and stop. | 2b<br>*Forces and their Effect Level A* | Finding objects in the classroom that require a push to move and objects that require a pull. Labelling them appropriately. Class or group activity. | 75 |
| *Pushes and pulls, page 75* | | | | |
| **Rock, swivel, spin and swing** | To describe the movement of familiar things. | 2a<br>*As above* | Investigating and observing items which demonstrate rocking, spinning or swivelling motions such as pendulums, rocking horses and swivel chairs. Small group practical activity. | 77 |
| *The everyday language of forces and motion, page 74* | | | | |

| ACTIVITY TITLE | LEARNING OBJECTIVE | POS/AO | CONTENT |
|---|---|---|---|
| **Shake, rattle and roll** | To describe how things move, speed up and change direction. | 2a<br>*Forces and their Effect Level A* | Investigating and observing the movement of dice and tiddlywinks when different forces are applied to them.<br>Class or group investigation. |
| **Fan the kipper** | To know that moving air is a force which makes things move. | 2b<br>*As above* | Making a paper 'kipper' or using the photocopiable template and investigating how it moves when it is fanned.<br>Class or group activity. |
| **Forces in a bottle** | Forces make things start, stop and change direction. | 2c<br>*As above* | Investigating the movement of bottles when they are part-filled with water. Considering the rocking movement.<br>Class introduction followed by group investigation. |
| **Run like the wind** | To know that the forces of pushes and pulls make things speed up, slow down and change direction. | 2c<br>*As above* | Investigating the wind as a pushing and pulling force. Class or group activity. |
| **Slow, slow, quick, quick, sideways, page 77** | | | |
| **The tube** | Some objects made from certain materials can have their shape changed by squashing, bending and twisting. Forces can change the shape of objects. | 2d<br>*Forces and their Effect Level A* | Considering different tube shapes and where they are found in the environment. Investigating what happens to a cardboard tube when it is twisted or squashed.<br>Class introduction followed by group investigation. |
| **Squeeze aquash and pummel, page 78** | | | |
| **Playing in the dark** | We need light in order to see things. | 3b<br>*Properties and Uses of Energy Level A* | Using different materials to make a dark place.<br>Class introduction followed by group activity. |
| **Sounds good page 83; Sounds all around, page 85; Sound moves, page 87** | | | |
| **The dragon's treasure** | There are many kinds of sound and we hear them when they enter the ear. | 3c 3e<br>*As above* | Playing a listening game. Pinpointing the direction of a sound.<br>Class activity. |

# Life processes and living things

The activities in this chapter encompass children's natural curiosity for the living world. The activities cover all aspects of life processes and living things and are taught through first-hand contexts so that children can learn through practical experience.

Due to the context of observing living things, teachers will need to deal sensitively with the issues of handling and disturbing creatures and plants. Due regard to health and safety issues should be made and it is recommended that each school's policy of going into the local environment to study is followed. The use of a well-developed conservation area would enhance many activities.

There are opportunities for the children to plan and carry out investigations and the range of investigative and experimental science skills are developed. The early skills of sorting, classifying, noticing similarities and differences, and making comparisons of size, shape, colour and texture are particularly well covered.

Parents can be encouraged to support many activities through support in the classroom, supervising and helping a group of children while carrying out their investigations, or through providing objects for the many collections that the children will use for the sorting activities in particular.

## SHOES

*We use our hands and fingers to find out by touching.*

†† *Whole class then individuals.*

🕐 *20 minutes.*

⚠ *Safety: Use footwear that does not have sharp fastenings.*

### Previous skills/knowledge needed

It would be useful if the children had already carried out a feely bag activity and were familiar with some of the language associated with the description of touch.

### Preparation

Obtain a large feely bag (pillowcase), or box (retail crisp box) large enough to hold a selection of footwear. You may wish to set up a shelf or interactive display space so that the activity can be repeated by individual children throughout the week. Gather together a wide variety of footwear in different sizes and shapes and made from materials that feel significantly different, for example wellington boots, slippers, sandals, lace-up shoes, flip-flops, slip-on plimsolls, and so on. Place one of each pair inside the bag or box. During the lesson, you will need to keep the other item in each pair beside you to show to the children. Make copies of photocopiable page 93, one for each child. If you wish to carry out the extension activity you will need to obtain pairs of socks in various fabrics with different types of motifs or patterns on them.

## Resources needed
A large feely bag or box, a selection of different types of footwear, blank paper/photocopiable page 93, writing materials. For the extension activity – pairs of different types of socks.

## Language to be introduced
Smooth, soft, hard, bendy, furry, rough, curved, square, straight, pointed, stretchy, texture.

## What to do
Gather the children together into a group and sit them in a circle. Place the feely bag or box containing one of each of the pairs of footwear in the centre of the circle. Select the wellington boot from your side and pass it around the circle so that each child has a chance to feel it. Ask the children to tell you something about what the wellington feels like. *Can you bend the wellington? Is it soft, hard, smooth? What can you say about its texture?*

Ask one child to feel inside the feely bag and to try to find the matching wellington. Place the pair of wellingtons on the shelf or display surface where all the children can see them. Continue in the same way with the other items of footwear you have collected until all the pairs have been successfully matched.

Hand out some blank paper and encourage the children to record the activity by drawing the pairs of shoes they have matched. Alternatively, give each child a copy of photocopiable page 93 if you have used the same types of footwear as the ones drawn on the sheet. Explain that this is a simple matching activity. The children must join each item of footwear at the top of the page to its partner.

## Suggestion(s) for extension
The children can play the same game but this time using pairs of socks which feel significantly different. Use socks made from different materials, with distinctive patterns or embroidered motifs that can easily be identified by using the sense of touch.

## Suggestion(s) for support
Some children may not have the language development necessary to describe the objects. Encourage these children to describe each item of footwear using their sense of sight, for example looking at the size and shape of the different shoes. Suggest some of the words they can use to describe how the footwear feels.

## Assessment opportunities
Make a note of those children who can easily match the pairs and move these children on to the extension activity. Those children whose language needs further development may benefit from doing

the activity in *Curriculum Bank Science, Key Stage One* entitled 'Feeling Surfaces' on page 14.

## Display ideas
Arrange each item of footwear and the feely bag or box along a display surface where the children can play the

game individually during the week. The sock game can be displayed in the same area by hanging a washing-line across a display board.

## Other aspects of the Science PoS covered
Experimental and Investigative Science 2a, 2b, 2c.

## Reference to photocopiable sheet
Photocopiable page 93 shows various items of footwear. The children have to link each item to its partner.

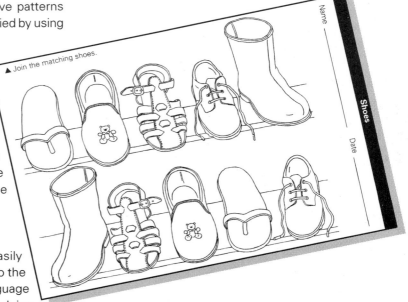
▲ Join the matching shoes.

# SQUIDGY FEELINGS!

*We use our sense of touch to find out some properties of foods.*

**†† ** *Groups of six children.*

**⊕** *30 minutes.*

**⚠** *Safety: Make sure the bags are tightly sealed so that the contents do not ooze out as they are squeezed. Remind the children that the food items are not to be eaten as the rules of hygiene and handling food have not been followed. Do not allow the foods to become contaminated or go rotten. Even though the food is not being used for tasting, do not use food items which children are allergic to. Follow your school's policy on this.*

## Key background information

This lesson links well with the activity 'Shoes' on page 12 of this book and 'Feeling surfaces' and 'Feely bags' on pages 14 and 15 of *Curriculum Bank Science, Key Stage One.*

## Preparation

You will need a range of materials to be felt which could include some pasta. Cook your pasta (al dente!) and prepare some feely bags or boxes. You can use any bag with a drawstring for a feely bag. Feely boxes can be made from empty cardboard boxes, such as crisp boxes. Cut a hole out of one side of the box and stick a flap of card or

strips of paper on the inside to cover the hole. Colour code the bags or boxes or, if appropriate, number them. In addition to preparing the feely bags themselves you will need to pre-pack the items to go in the feely bags by putting them in separate, tightly sealed, non-transparent freezer bags. Make copies of photocopiable pages 94 and 95 for those children carrying out the extension activity.

## Resources needed

Feely bags or boxes, a range of feely substances which could include: cooked pasta, baked beans, a vegetable samosa, rice, a bread roll and a bag of sand. The list should be varied if this activity is to be repeated by different groups through the week. On different days you could include: pitta bread, a crusty bread roll, a rock, tinned pineapples (drained), a bag of flour, a mango and so on. For the extension activity – photocopiable pages 94 and 95, gloves, writing and drawing materials.

## Language to be introduced

Sense, touch, feel, hard, solid, squashy, flexible. This lesson can generate a great deal of language work and the precise vocabulary required is hard to predict.

## What to do

Show the children the feely bag or box and explain that you are going to put a bag inside for them to feel. Tell the children that all the bags, apart from one, contain food. It is their job to try to identify the bag which does not contain food. Explain that they are not allowed to peep inside the bags but must use their sense of touch.

At this point, ask the children to close their eyes while you put one bag inside the feely bag or box. Invite one child to feel the item inside the bag and record the findings with him or her. *What does it feel like? Is it soft or squidgy? Is it hard or runny?* Now ask the child to guess what the

bag contains. If you have a group of six children and six bags you can give them one each to investigate in more detail. Tremendous language work can be derived from pairing the children at this stage, asking them to agree on the contents of the bag before reporting back their findings to the rest of the group.

To round off the activity, help the children reflect on their sense of touch more generally. Which parts of their hands did they use to explore the contents of the feely bags? Which parts of their hands are the most/least sensitive? What other parts of their bodies are sensitive to touch? Some children will talk about their feet and other body parts which are ticklish. In the past this has led some pupils into discussions about 'good and bad touches'. Consequently, this part of the lesson may need to be handled sensitively.

Finally, you may wish to make use of the language which has been generated in this activity by writing a 'Squidgy-Squashy' poem.

### Suggestion(s) for extension
If some children find the task too simple, dull their sense of touch by asking them to identify objects or materials while wearing gloves. Ask the children to try to map their hands or feet for touch-sensitive areas. Provide the children with a feather or cotton bud so that they can locate the most and least sensitive parts. This can often be very funny but will need extra supervision. Next, the children should draw around their hands or feet and use the outline as a 'map'. Alternatively, they can use photocopiable pages 94 and 95. The children can record the sensitivity of the different areas of their hands and feet by colouring those areas with little feeling in red, those areas with some feeling in orange and those areas with lots of feeling in green. The children may suggest alternative colours.

### Suggestion(s) for support
Some children may need more experience of using their sense of touch in practical investigations. A sand or salt tray is good for drawing and letter formation. Also, give children objects to identify with their hands behind their backs, play blindfold games, and so on.

### Assessment opportunities
As the children try to identify the contents of the feely bags, make a special note of those children who give focused answers. Look out for children who are very wide of the mark when describing the contents of the bags. Is there anyone who is feeling a solid shape and describing it as a liquid? The bag of sand often causes confusion here.

### Display ideas
The feely bags are an interactive display in their own right. Add question cards to challenge the children such as: 'Can you guess what is inside this bag?' Or use prompts such as: 'Use your sense of touch to find out what is inside these bags...'. Children often generate their own descriptive words during this lesson. These can be displayed alongside more conventional descriptive phrases and words to enhance the children's sense of ownership of the activity. Display the feely bags around the children's 'Squidgy-Squashy' poem.

### Other aspects of the Science PoS covered
Materials and their Properties lb, 2a. Section 0 1b, 2b.

### Reference to photocopiable sheets
Photocopiable pages 94 and 95 contain the outlines of the front and back of a hand and the upper part and sole of a foot. Using different colours, the children must colour in the different parts of the hands and feet according to their sensitivity.

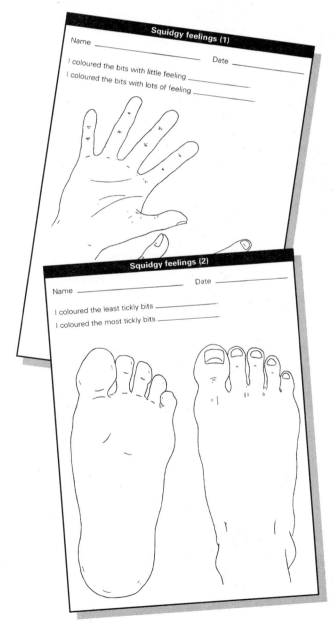

# TICKLING TOES

*We can use our feet for feeling.*

†† *Whole class then groups.*

🕐 *30 minutes.*

⚠ *Safety: Make sure all the floor samples are free from sharp edges and splinters.*

## Previous skills/knowledge needed

It would be useful if the children had completed an activity to develop the appropriate vocabulary, for example the activity 'Feeling surfaces' on page 14 of *Curriculum Bank Science, Key Stage One*.

## Preparation

Collect a number of floorings and mats with different surfaces and cut them to similar sizes big enough for children to feel with their feet. A range from some of the following would be ideal: carpet square, vinyl flooring, ceramic tile, Marley tile, foam underlay, parquet flooring, rubber, coconut, rush and plastic doormats. Cut a piece of each sample into squares measuring 8cm × 6 cm for the children to stick on to the photocopiable sheet. Make sufficient copies of photocopiable page 96, one for each child. Make either individual copies of the wordlist on photocopiable page 97, or enlarged copies, one for each group. You may also need to brief an adult helper to work with those children carrying out the support activity.

## Resources needed

A selection of different floor samples, writing materials, paste, photocopiable pages 96 and 97, sorting rings, labels. For the extension activity – a blindfold.

## Language to be introduced

Rough, smooth, soft, hard, warm, cold, furry, hairy, bumpy, squashy, prickly, bristly, itchy, fluffy, tickly, lumpy.

## What to do

Spread the different types of flooring out on a carpet or similar area in the classroom. Gather the children together and sit them in a circle around the samples of flooring. Briefly discuss the floorings with the children. What are they called? Do the children have any of these types of flooring in their homes? Have they seen the floorings in shops or in school? Are the types of flooring found inside or outside the buildings? Are they usually found in certain rooms and not in others? Explain to the children that in order to find out about the different flooring samples, they are going to feel the various textures using their big toes.

Ask one child to remove his or her socks and shoes and to use his or her big toe to feel a piece of flooring. Ask the child to think of words to describe what the flooring feels like. Is it smooth, hard, soft, rough, prickly? Invite another child to feel the floor sample. Can he or she think of other words to describe it? Continue until all of the samples have been described in this way.

Now the children are ready to play a guessing game. Explain to the children the rules of the game and how important it is that they do not cheat by peeping. Tell them that they are all going to close their eyes except for one child who is going to choose one sample of flooring, feel it with his or her big toe and describe what it feels like. The other children must not look! Instead they must try to work out from the description which sample of flooring the child was feeling. The child who guesses correctly selects the next piece of flooring to describe to the rest of the class.

After the children have played the game, organize them into groups and hand out copies of photocopiable page 96 to each child. Also give out copies of the wordlist on photocopiable page 97. Show them the small pieces of flooring you have prepared and explain that they must choose three samples of flooring and then stick these onto their sheet in the spaces that have been provided. They should then choose two words from the wordlist that best describes the texture of their chosen samples. (The children may prefer to think of their own words. The wordlist is provided as a prompt for the children.)

## Suggestion(s) for extension

Play the blindfold game. Blindfold a child and lead him or her carefully to a selected floor sample and ask the child to feel it with his or her foot. Can the child guess which

## Display ideas
Display the samples of flooring with labels containing the children's suggestions for describing their textures. Alternatively, you can set up an interactive display with the samples, labels and sorting rings so that the children can sort the samples during the week. Each day display a different 'Guess the flooring' riddle for the children to solve such as: I am prickly, hard and itchy. I am good for cleaning mud off shoes. What am I?

## Other aspects of the Science PoS covered
Experimental and Investigative Science 2a, 2b, 2c.

## Reference to photocopiable sheets
Photocopiable page 96 is a recording sheet on which the children can stick various samples of flooring. They should then write two describing words next to each sample. Photocopiable page 97 is a wordlist containing words likely to be introduced during the activity. This can be enlarged for group or classroom display use, or reduced and mounted on card for individual spelling sheets. The words are numbered to support improving readers.

sample he or she is feeling? Alternatively, the children can be asked to sort the samples into sets of different textures.

## Suggestion(s) for support
Ask an adult helper to work with small groups of children to develop the appropriate language before they play the blindfold game. Limit the range of floorings, for example furry and not furry; smooth and rough. Ask the children to put all the furry samples in one pile and the non-furry ones in another. Continue until you have introduced all the describing words that you would like the children to know. Ask them to select the flooring sample that would be best in the bedroom. Can they say why? For example, the carpet would be good because it is warm, soft to bare feet and comfortable to the touch.

## Assessment opportunities
Make a note of those children who are able to describe and recognize the floorings using the appropriate language with confidence. Which children can use their knowledge and understanding to identify and/or sort the samples according to their textures?

## Opportunities for IT
The children could use a simple database package to survey the school for 'Surfaces we like to walk on with bare feet'. The information can be used to display the children's preferences.

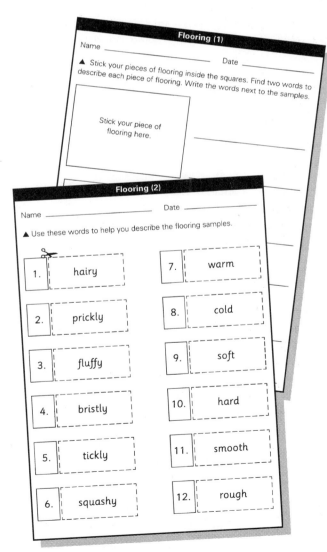

# MATCH MY SOUND

*We use our sense of hearing to find out about the world.*

†† *Class introduction followed by individual or paired activity.*

⏱ *30 minutes.*

⚠ *Safety: If small objects are used, remind the children that if the contents come out of the pot they should tell you straight away and not put anything into small body holes!*

### Previous skills/knowledge needed

It may be useful to have completed a sound source identification activity such as 'Exploring sound' on page 18 of *Curriculum Bank Science, Key Stage One*.

### Preparation

Prepare a set of matching sound pots – cover some yoghurt pots or disposable cups with greaseproof paper attached with elastic bands. Alternatively, you may like to use matching pots with lids; cake decoration pots or film containers are ideal. Fill each pair of pots with identical amounts of objects that make the same sounds. Suitable objects include dried peas, rice, sand, scrunched-up paper, sequins, paper-clips and salt. Stick a different coloured sticker to each pot to aid recording. Make copies of photocopiable page 98, one for each child. Make an enlarged copy for demonstration with the class.

### Resources needed

Disposable cups/yoghurt pots, elastic bands and greaseproof paper, or pots with lids. Rice, sand, salt, dried peas, sequins, paper-clips, scrunched-up paper, coloured stickers. Drawing materials (make sure you have the same colours as the stickers). Photocopiable page 98, plus an enlarged copy.

### Language to be introduced

Match, sound, listen, hear, soft, loud, harsh, scrape, scratch.

### What to do

For the introduction to this activity, use three pairs of matching sound pots only. Gather the children together so that they can all hear the sounds in the pots. Choose one pot and ask a child to shake it. Invite the other children to describe the sound they are hearing. *Is it a quiet/soft/ loud/harsh sound?* When you are sure that the children are able to recognize the sound again, invite another child to shake a different pot. Ask the children whether this pot makes the same sound as the first one. Are they able to say whether it does or not and, more importantly, give good reasons for their opinions? Continue to shake each pot until all the pots have been described. Some children

may already have noticed that some of the pots make the same sound. If not, explain at this point that some of the pots make identical sounds and that you are going to play a snap game with the pots. Tell the children they must use their sense of hearing to identify which pots make the same sound. Ask one child to choose two pots and to shake them one after the other. When both pots have been shaken, the children should decide whether the pots make the same sound. If they do, then the children should shout 'snap'. If they do not, invite another child to choose two pots and to shake them one after the other. Continue like this until the children have successfully matched the three sets of pots.

At this point, show the children the different-coloured stickers on each pot. Shake a matching pair of pots and show the children the two different colours on the side of the pots. Using your enlarged copy of photocopiable page 98, show the children how they can record which pots match by colouring the stickers on the sheet in the corresponding colours. Give each child a copy of photocopiable page 98 and explain that you are going to put some more pots on the sound table so that the children can play this game individually or with a friend. The pots can then be displayed as part of an interactive display for the children to investigate further.

## Suggestion(s) for extension

Encourage the children to make their own matching pots for their friends to match. They may be able to investigate the variables necessary for making identical sounds, for example, that they must use the same textured materials, and the same amount of the same material. Can they make matching sound pots using different materials or do they always need the same materials? Musical instruments can be introduced to compare the sounds they make. For instance, you can ask the children to put a set of chime bars in order, sequencing them from low to high sounds and so on.

## Suggestion(s) for support

Be sensitive to those children who may have a hearing impairment. The use of a microphone and amplifiers may be appropriate depending on the child. An additional adult who can play the game again on a one-to-one basis will help these children.

## Assessment opportunities

It is important that the children are able to understand that the use of their sense of hearing plays an important part in the development of their investigative skills. Make a note of those children who are able to recognize this and who make a real effort to use their sense of hearing to match the pots.

## Opportunities for IT

The children may like to record the sounds of the various objects and their responses using a tape recorder.

## Display ideas

An interactive sounds display can be set up whereby the children can match their own and others' matching sound pots. You may wish to change these on a daily basis although you will eventually runout of ideas for the contents of the pots. However, children will often make suggestions themselves. You may wish to set up a tape recorder with a 'Guess what is making this sound' tape.

## Other aspects of the Science PoS covered

Experimental and Investigative Science 2a, 2b, 2c, 3a, 3b, 3c, 3d, 3f. Physical Processes 3e.

## Reference to photocopiable sheet

Photocopiable page 98 is a simple recording sheet which will provide evidence of those children who can successfully use their sense of hearing to find out which pots make the same sound. The children should record the colours of the matching sound pots and then link each pair by drawing a line between them.

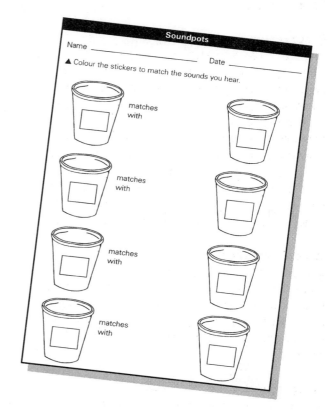

# IDENTIFYING ARCHIE

***We use our eyes or sense of sight to notice detail and help us find out about things around us.***

†† *Class or individual activity.*

🕐 *30 minutes.*

⚠ *Safety: Use objects which are safe to handle. Avoid objects with sharp edges and points such as scissors, pins and needles.*

## Preparation

Make three collections of objects.

▲ Set 1 should contain a variety of different objects.

▲ Set 2 should contain different varieties of apples (one apple of each variety but excluding the variety used in set 3).

▲ Set 3 should contain apples of the same variety.

Make copies of photocopiable page 99, one for each child.

## Resources needed

A set of significantly different objects, one apple of several varieties which look and feel very different (Russet, Golden Delicious, Granny Smiths, Cox's are good choices) several apples of the same variety, photocopiable page 99, drawing materials. For the extension activity – blank paper.

## Language to be introduced

Same, different, blemish, bump, round, flat, shape, smooth, rough, spotty, stalk, core, peel, scar, mark.

## What to do

Gather the children together and tell them the story of Archie. Pick an apple from set 3 and tell the children that this is Archie. Archie is an apple who loves playing 'Hide and Seek' with his best friend Fred (or any name you wish to insert depending on the ethnic mix and so on of the children in your class). Fred can be a person, another fruit type or even another apple. You or the children can decide. Tell the children that Archie is always looking for good places to hide so that Fred cannot find him. One day Archie decided to hide in this group of objects. At this point introduce the set of different objects (set 1) and place Archie in the middle of them. Ask the children whether they think this is a good place for Archie to hide. Do they think it is easy for Fred to find Archie? Hopefully, they will express the opinion that it is not a very good place to hide because it is very easy to spot Archie. Spend some time discussing how Archie is different to the other objects in the set. *Is there anything about the objects and Archie that is the same?* After a suitable discussion period, continue with the story. Archie decides to hide in a different place and he is determined to make it impossible for Fred to find him. At this point introduce set 2. Ask the children whether they think this is a better place for Archie to hide. *Will Fred find it easy to find Archie now? Why?* Again the children should find it quite easy to pick out Archie from the apples in this set because although the set contains different varieties of apples, they still all look very different from each other.

Discuss some of the similarities and differences between the apples in set 2. Tell the children to use their eyes and sense of sight to observe the colour, size, shape, texture and blemishes on the apples. Again, when you feel it is appropriate, continue with the story. Archie decides to have one more go to try and hide from Fred. He is really determined that Fred will not find him this time! At this point introduce the set of apples which are

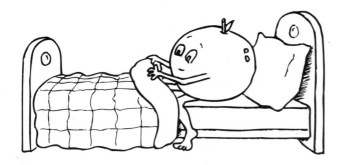

all the same variety as Archie (set 3). You can have as many or as few apples in the set as you wish, depending on the age and abilities of the children in the class or group. Can the children still find Archie? Can they still be sure that the apple they have chosen is Archie? How do they know? Will it be easy for Fred to find Archie? The children should use their sense of sight to identify the similarities and differences between Archie and the other apples in the set. At this point, show the children photocopiable page 99 and explain that they are going to compare Archie with one of the other apples. Place Archie in the centre of the class so that all the children can see the apple. Explain that they should use their sense of sight to record the colour, texture and blemishes of Archie. Invite the children to choose another apple from set 3 and explain that they should record the features of this apple in the second apple shape provided. They may wish to give this apple a name also!

## Suggestion(s) for extension

Give each child carrying out the extension activity an apple of the same variety to look after for the morning. Tell them that they are going to play a game in which they pretend that their apple needs a lot of care. Encourage them to cuddle the apple so that they learn about it using their sense of touch. Ask them to draw their apples and to describe them to a friend. They may even want to make their apples a comfortable bed! At lunchtime tell the children to put their apples together in a box. When they return in the afternoon ask the children whether they can find their apples. How do they know they have picked their apple and not someone else's? The activity can be made even harder by asking the children to describe their apple to a friend. Can their friend select the correct apple from the box using the information given?

## Suggestion(s) for support

Some children may need additional help identifying similarities and differences in order to find Archie from the objects in sets 1 and 2. Use photocopiable page 99 but complete the colour and blemishes of Archie together. Draw their attention to specific spots, rough patches, bruises, length and colour of stalk, colour and bumps and

show them where to record the information on Archie's apple shape. They can then complete the recording of a second apple on the other outline provided. Encourage the children to note the different colours and blemishes on the apples. Further discussions should reinforce the learning objective: that they have used their eyes and sense of sight to observe the different features of an object and thus to identify things about that object.

## Assessment opportunities

It is important that the children develop the skill of being able to identify similarities and differences in order to develop their observation skills. Make a note of those children who are able to use this skill to give appropriate reasons as to whether it is easy or difficult to find Archie in each of the sets of objects.

## Display ideas

The children can write their descriptions of Archie on apple-shaped cutouts and display these on a tree. Alternatively, a daily interactive display can be set up so that the children can find Archie among a changing set of objects which increase in difficulty as the weeks progress.

## Other aspects of the Science PoS covered

Experimental and investigative science 2a, 2b, 2c, 3a, 3c. Section 0 4a, 4b.

## Reference to photocopiable sheet

Photocopiable page 99 contains two outlines of apples in which the children record the different colours and blemishes of 'Archie' and another apple.

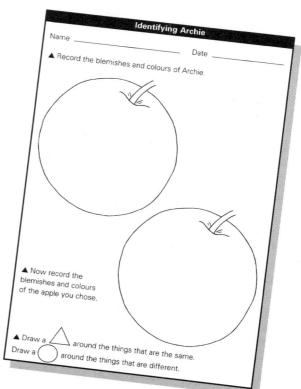

# FIND MY COLOUR

*We use our sense of sight to find out about the world around us.*

✝✝ *Class introduction followed by a group activity.*

🕐 *45 minutes.*

⚠️ *Safety: If you are going outside the school environment you may need some adult helpers. All offsite visits should be carried out in accordance with school guidelines. Be sensitive to any children who are colour blind and ensure that they are not given strips containing red, green or brown tones.*

## Preparation

Make some colour strips so that there are adequate strips for each child. Seal the paint, for example with PVA glue, so that the paint does not stain hands and clothing. For the main activity, the strips should be varied and contain colours that are very different. You will also need a selection of strips that contain shades, tones and tints of the same colour. Make sure that some of the colours you choose will easily match items that can be found in the classroom. Preferably, use a good quality card which is small enough for the children to hold in one hand and which will not flop over when held. You may wish to use commercially produced charts which are available from any good DIY store. As you will be taking groups of children outside you will also need extra classroom assistance.

## Resources needed

Paint colour chart or strips, some with very different colours on each strip and some with shades of the same colour.

## Language to be introduced

Tones, tints, shade, match, light, dark.

## What to do

Select one of the colour strips making sure that it contains the colours of some of the items in the classroom. Talk to the children about the colour strip you have chosen. Ask them whether they can find something in the classroom that is the same, or nearly the same, colour shade as one of the shades on the strip. Tell them to look around the classroom and to suggest items that have the same colour match. Encourage them to explain their choices in ways such as: *The carpet is the same greeny, bluey shade as this colour. The leaves on the plant are a yellowy, greeny colour like this one.* Next, ask each child to choose one of the colour strips. Stress that they will need to make a careful choice because they are going to go outside into the playground to look for things in the environment that match the colours on the strip they have chosen. Explain that they are going to use their sense of sight; they will be looking very carefully at the things outside to learn about the world around them. Remind the children at this stage about the school's rules of behaviour and safety.

Allow the children a few minutes to select their colour strip before taking them outside in groups of six or eight to look for things which match the colours on their chosen strip.

After about 15 minutes return to the classroom and gather the class together on the carpet. (Younger children may take less time outside.) Ask the children about their discoveries.

▲ *What things did you find?*

▲ *Who found something that was yellow/red/blue/green/*

grey/orange?

▲ Who found something that was a really interesting colour?

▲ Who found a colour on their colour strip which matched the blossom on the cherry tree/the grass/the petals on the daffodils?

▲ Who found lots of things that matched the colours on their strip?

▲ Who found it difficult to find things to match the colours on their strip?

▲ Who can tell me why some children found lots of things and some children found hardly anything?

If the children are able, spend a few minutes discussing why some found it easier than others to find things in the environment which matched the colours on their colour strip. Emphasize the learning objective: that they have learned to look very carefully to find out about the colours of things in their environment.

### Suggestion(s) for extension

Use shades of green on the cards to match with natural objects. Tell the children to collect a selection of green leaves. They should then press them and observe any changes of colour over a period of time.

### Suggestion(s) for support

Limit the selection of colours on the strips and ensure the colours on each strip are very different from each other. Encourage the children to find things that match the colour

rather than a shade. For example, they should notice that the leaves on the tree are green and not worry about the shade of green. The activity can form part of a series of activities to be repeated during the week.

### Assessment opportunities

Make a note of those children who show an awareness of shades of colour and are developing their observational skills to learn and find out more about the world around them.

### Opportunities for IT

Investigate the shades of colour available on a Paint program and use it to make a pattern of colours. Use different colours with younger children. Older or more able children will be able to select shades of the same colour.

### Display ideas

The children can make their own colour strips. These can then be used to make a collage of the things they found outside, using the colour strips to match the colours as closely as they can. Alternatively, they may wish to draw a large picture of their playground onto which they can display individual cut-out pictures of the things they matched to their colour strips.

### Other aspects of the Science PoS covered

Section 0 1b, 1c, 2a, 2c, 5b.
Experimental and Investigative Science 2a, 2b, 2c, 3a, 3c.

# COLOURED MILK

*Our mouths and tongues give us a sense of taste which helps us to make decisions about flavours.*

†† *Individual within groups of four to eight.*

🕐 *45 minutes.*

⚠ *Safety: Check that no child has an allergy to colourings or milk. Semi or skimmed milk would support any teaching objectives to promote a healthy diet. It may be appropriate to send out a letter to all parents asking for information about any allergies from which their child may suffer. Make sure that all hygiene procedures as laid down by your school's policy are followed.*

### Previous skills/knowledge needed

Before attempting this activity, it is necessary to have carried out an activity identifying different flavours such as 'Taste' on page 18 of *Curriculum Bank Science, Key Stage One*.

### Key background information

This activity will help children to understand that even though the milk in the different containers looks different, it will in fact taste the same. The children are relying only on their sense of taste to make a decision about the flavours.

### Preparation

Before the start of the lesson, pour small amounts of milk into four disposable cups and cover them with clingfilm. Make copies of photocopiable pages 100 for those children carrying out the main activity. Make copies of photocopiable page 101 for those children carrying out the support activity.

### Resources needed

Four disposable cups, clingfilm, enough straws for every child to have one each, fresh milk, red, yellow, green and blue colourings, four droppers (one for each colouring), photocopiable page 100, writing and drawing materials. For the support activity – photocopiable page 101.

### Language to be introduced

Predict, taste, colouring, flavour.

### What to do

Gather the children around a table where you have placed the four cups containing milk. Explain to the children that you are going to add a different colouring to each of the cups. Depending on the age and ability of the children, you may wish to discuss with them the fact that you are going to be very careful to add the same amount of colouring to each cup. Now add a very small amount of each of the colourings in equal quantities to the cups so that you have red (or pink), yellow, green, and blue coloured milk. Ask the children which milk they think will taste the nicest. Stress that they are predicting which milk they think will have the best flavour not their favourite colour! Give each child a copy of photocopiable page 100 on which to record their choice. Encourage them to give reasons for their choice; their responses will be very interesting. The photocopiable sheet can also be used as a tick or tally chart onto which the children can record the predictions and choices of their classmates during the activity.

When the children have done this, spend some time discussing the reasons for their choices. Some children will choose a colour because it reminds them of their favourite flavoured milks such as strawberry, mint or banana. Discuss whether the milk will taste of a particular flavour. Ask the children whether you added any strawberries, mint or banana to the milks and emphasize that only colours were added. Some children will choose their favourite colour. Discuss whether the colour will change the taste of the milk. Next, tell the children to taste each of the four coloured milks. When each child has had a sip, ask them which one tasted the best. The children can use the bottom half of photocopiable page 100 to record their personal response and to ask the same children they questioned originally what their opinions are after tasting.

Some children will use their sense of taste to conclude that all the milks taste the same, others will stick to their original prediction because they do not wish to be proved wrong. The responses will help you assess how well the children are able to use results to draw conclusions. Once all the children have tasted the milk, tell them that you had tried to trick them but they had been very clever and used their sense of taste to find out that although the milk in the cups looked different, they all tasted the same.

### Suggestion(s) for extension

Some children will be able to record all the children's predictions and choices on a block graph using the data recorded on photocopiable page 100. Encourage them to analyse the information to find out which colouring was predicted the most/least often. They can then compare the results with their predictions.

## Display ideas

The children's written reports of their investigation, or their responses on photocopiable pages 100 and 101, can be displayed as part of a display on taste.

## Other aspects of the Science PoS covered

Experimental and Investigative Science 2a, 2b, 2c, 3a, 3b, 3c, 3d, 3e, 3f. Section 0 1b, 1d, 2b, 3a, 4b, 5b.

## Reference to photocopiable sheets

Photocopiable page 100 is a tick or tally chart. The children use it both before and after tasting to note down predictions and conclusions about which milk will taste the best. Photocopiable page 101 is a simpler recording sheet for those children needing extra support. It requires them to colour in the picture of the glass of milk and then to complete a sentence about what they have found out after they have tasted the milk.

## Suggestion(s) for support

Some children may find it difficult to understand that the different cups of milk will taste the same because the colourings have no taste. It is important that these children take part in all discussions and listen to what other children think. However, do not push them into accepting the concept, instead repeat the activity at a later date when you think they are ready to understand. You may also like to give these children copies of photocopiable page 101 rather than page 100 to complete. This is a simpler sheet which requires them to colour in the picture of the glass of milk and then to complete a sentence about their findings.

## Assessment opportunities

It is important to make a note of those children who can predict and understand that although the milk looks different it will taste the same. These children have learned to use their sense of taste to inform their decisions about flavours. How many children are able to discuss the evidence realistically and say whether it supports any predictions made?

## Opportunities for IT

A simple Graphit program can be used to input the children's predictions and choices. The graph can be saved and retrieved at a later date to input any additional information gathered. Some software programs will allow you to order and display the information in a different format.

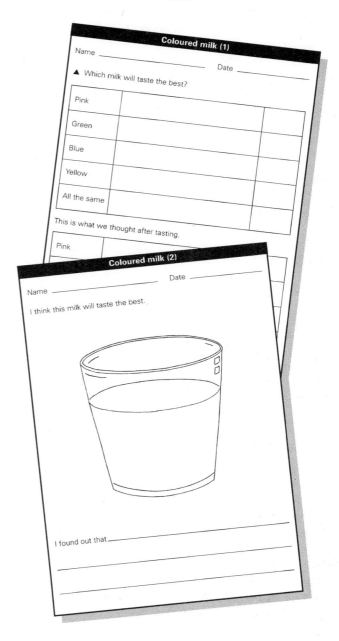

# WHO AM I?

*Some things about us are different and some are the same.*

†† *Class activity.*

🕐 *20 minutes.*

⚠ *Safety: Be aware of the issues associated with bullying in this activity. You will need to monitor very carefully that children are not referring to physical characteristics in a disparaging way.*

## Previous skills/knowledge needed

The children should be able to name the different parts of the body and facial features.

## Preparation

Plan a series of criteria to match to the children in your class, for example eye colour, hair colour, freckles. Decide on some children beforehand who you will match to various criteria (see 'What to do'). Make copies of photocopiable page 102 for those children carrying out the main activity. Make copies of photocopiable page 103 for those children carrying out the support activity.

## Resources needed

Photocopiable page 102, writing and drawing materials. For the support activity – photocopiable page 103.

## Language to be introduced

Hair colours, for example, fair, auburn, brown, blonde; eye colours, for example, green, hazel, blue, brown; taller, shorter, male, female, glasses, same, different.

## What to do

Gather the children together and explain that you are going to play a game which will teach them that they all have some things about themselves which are the same but other things which are different. For example, some children have brown eyes, some have green eyes, some have blue eyes and so on. Do not labour the point at this stage but start the following activity.

Ask all the children to stand up in the centre of the working space. Explain that you are going to describe some features which some children have but that others do not. Ask all the children who have, for example, blue eyes to stand to one side of the main group so that they are separated. Explain that this group of children have something about them which is the same. They all have blue eyes. The other group are therefore different from the first group in at least one way; they do not have blue eyes. Say something like: *This group are different because they do not have blue eyes.* Tell this group to sit down and concentrate on the group with blue eyes. Next, ask all the children with blonde hair to stand apart from the group. Explain that the children in this group have at least two

things about them which is the same: they all have blue eyes and blonde hair. The blue eyes are one feature and the blonde hair is another. Does this group have any other features which are the same? Spend only a small amount of time discussing this.

Now begin to play the main game. Tell the children in the various groups to rejoin the others. Tell the children that you are thinking of a child in the class. Their job is to work out who you are thinking of from the descriptions you give. Begin by saying something like: *I am thinking of someone with brown hair. Therefore if you have brown hair it could be you!* Ask all the children with brown hair to stand to one side. Direct the children's attention to this group and say: *I am thinking of someone with brown hair and hazel eyes. Therefore, if you have brown hair and hazel eyes, stand here!* Direct this smaller group of children to one side away from the group and tell those children left in the brown hair group to rejoin the rest of the class.

Direct the children's attention to the smaller group of children and say: *I am thinking of a person who has brown hair, hazel eyes and who is female. Therefore if you have brown hair, hazel eyes and are female, please come and stand by me.* (It may be necessary to qualify the meaning of any descriptors the children do not understand as you proceed with this activity.) Next, ask the children to look closely at the small group of children you have remaining at this point. Explain that all these children have at least three things about them which are the same but there are still some differences. Ask: *Can anyone think of a different feature that can be included to eliminate a few more children?* You may wish to continue until all but one of the children have been eliminated.

At some point you will probably need to explain to the children that things such as the colour of clothing cannot be included as these are not part of our personal features, they are not part of us. We can put them on or off whereas we cannot (hopefully!) put our hair on and off. You may have to debate whether glasses should be included. A rule you may like to use is that if the glasses are worn all of the time, they can be included; if they are worn only on certain occasions, then they cannot. Play this game until you are sure that the children understand the concepts involved. You may find that it is necessary to play it over a number of days or even weeks, perhaps at the end of storytime or a similar session. Eventually, you will find that the children are playing the game unprompted.

When you are sure that they understand the game, give each child a copy of photocopiable page 102 for them to complete. The children should imagine two people, or choose two children in the class, and then record three things that are the same, for example eye colour, hair length and skin tone, and three things that are different, for example, hair colour, glasses and freckles. This reinforces the learning objective that some things about us are the same and some things are different.

### Suggestion(s) for extension

You may wish to introduce more variables into this activity. The game 'Guess who?' is excellent for extending this concept and can be used within a series of activities with little supervision. You or a child select a person in the class but do not tell the class who you are thinking of. To work out who you are thinking of, the children must ask questions such as:

*Does the person have blue eyes?* Replies are given as only 'yes' or 'no' answers. The children sort themselves into the right groups depending on the answers until all but one child is eliminated.

### Suggestion(s) for support

An activity which involves collecting information on specific characteristics such as eye and hair colour would reinforce this concept and the understanding of 'same' and 'different'. Give children requiring extra support copies of photocopiable page 103. This is a 'Spot the difference' game for the children to create for a friend. The children draw two faces with various differences. The sheet is then passed to a friend who has to mark all the features on the second face that are different from the first.

### Assessment opportunities

The children's completed copies of photocopiable page 102 will provide evidence of those children who are able to identify that people have some things about them which are the same and other things which are different. This information can be used to assess which children are ready to work with similarities and differences between plants and animals and apply this knowledge and understanding to the study of habitats.

### Opportunities for IT

Draw a picture of a person or face using a simple graphics package which will allow the children to change the colour, size and shape of the features. Their picture can be saved and printed alongside the original picture and used as a 'Spot the difference' game.

### Display ideas

Draw around two children who are different in some ways and the same in others. Cut out the models and paint them

in appropriate colours. Display these with appropriate labels drawing attention to the things that are the same and the things that are different.

## Other aspects of the Science PoS covered

Experimental and Investigative Science 1a, 2b, 3c, 3f. Section 0 1d, 2c, 3a, 4a, 4b.

## Reference to photocopiable sheets

Photocopiable page 102 provides an illustration of two faces onto which the children must record three things that are the same and three things that are different. Photocopiable page 103 is a 'Spot the difference' game for the children to make themselves. The children should complete the faces, deciding on the various similarities and differences they wish to incorporate.

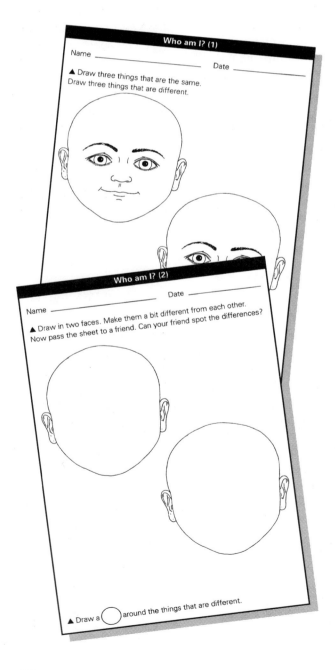

# ARE THESE MY HANDS?

**We all grow.**

†† Group activity within class lesson.

🕐 30 minutes.

## Preparation

Make photocopies of the front and back of each child's hand and several adults and older children known to them. Make a photocopy of your hand. Number the photocopies and keep a list of whose hand matches the numbered photocopies. If possible, obtain copies of babies hands although pictures cut from magazines, if large enough, will be suitable. Make copies of photocopiable page 104 for those children carrying out the extension activity.

## Resources needed

Photocopies of children's, adults' and babies' hands. For the extension activity – photocopiable page 104, writing materials.

## Language to be introduced

Big, bigger, biggest; small, smaller, smallest; long, longer, longest; short, shorter, shortest; fat, fatter, fattest; adult, grown-up, child, teenager, grow, centimetre.

## What to do

Show the children a photocopy of your hand. (Do not tell them it is your hand at this stage.) Ask them what they can tell you about the picture. Draw their attention to the size of the fingers, their length and thickness, the position of the knuckles, the pattern of lines. Can the children describe the shape of the hand? Ask them whether they think it is the hand of a grown-up, a baby or a child. How do they know? There are a number of possible ways of surmising whether it is a baby's, child's or adult's hand but the important learning point is that the hands of an adult are bigger than the hands of a baby because we all grow.

Play a sorting game with the children. Organize the children into groups and give each group a set of photocopies of hands of different age-groups. Include the photocopies of the children's own hands. Can they find the photocopy of their own hand? How do they know it is their hand? Next, ask the children to group the hands into order according to the age of the owners. Encourage them to think about the shape and size of the hands. Talk about the reasons why the children have sorted the hands in the way they have. Check that the children who are able to do this are aware that we all grow until we become adults.

## Suggestion(s) for extension

The children could investigate aspects of growth. For example, is the left hand bigger than the right hand? Are

boys' hands bigger than girls' hands? Do grown ups' hands keep growing? Are mens' hands bigger than women's hands? Encourage the more able children to measure the hands using standardized measurements of centimetres and to measure the length of each hand from the top of the middle finger to the base of the hand. They can also measure the span of each hand (the distance between the little finger and thumb of an outstretched hand). How many pennies, for example, are needed to cover each hand. The information can be recorded using photocopiable page 104. This is a simple recording sheet on which the

fingers, thumbs and hands. They can discuss the quality of the photocopies and improve them by experimenting with the darkness, pressure of body part on the screen, and so on.

### Display ideas

Display the hands on a washing line across the classroom or a notice board where the children can see them clearly. The children can then order the hands according to age and play a spot your hand game. Photocopy the hands on green paper and make a picture of a Christmas tree. It works if everyone lends a hand!

### Other aspects of the Science PoS covered

Experimental and Investigative Science 2b, 2c, 3a, 3c, 3d, 3f. Section 0 1d, 4b.

### Reference to photocopiable sheet

Photocopiable page 104 provides a block graph onto which the children can record the measurements of various hands.

children can record the sizes of up to ten hands to help them make simple comparisons. Make one photocopy and add the chosen measurement to the horizontal axis before making copies for the class or group.

### Suggestion(s) for support

Some children may need support putting the hands into order of size. They may have to cut around the hands and place the cut-out of one hand on top of another in order to decide. The language of comparative size – bigger and biggest – should be reinforced at the same time.

### Assessment opportunities

Make a note of those children who are able to do this activity because they understand the concept that we all grow. Some children may find this activity too difficult and may benefit from the activity 'Growing children' in Curriculum Bank Science, Key Stage One, page 29.

### Opportunities for IT

The children could be taught how to use the photocopier. They can then produce a collection of body parts such as

# HEALTHY FOOD PLATES

*We eat different types of food, and eating the right types and amounts of food helps to keep us healthy.*

†† *Class then small groups.*

🕐 *30 minutes.*

⚠ *Safety: Explain to the children that they are going to be using pretend food and that they must not eat it.*

## Previous skills/knowledge needed

It would be useful if the children had completed the activity entitled 'Health and happiness' in *Curriculum Bank Science, Key Stage One,* page 24, or an activity looking at the food they had for breakfast, lunch or dinner. Briefly discuss the different types of food eaten in each meal.

## Preparation

Collect magazines and other publications containing pictures of food. You may wish to organize and brief an additional adult to support the main part of the activity.

## Resources needed

Paper plates, pictures of food (these can either be cut out or contained in magazines), plastic fruit/food items which can be purchased from educational catalogues, apple, packet of crisps, cream cake, paper, writing and drawing materials.

## Language to be introduced

Healthy, less healthy, fat, protein, sugar, vitamins.

## What to do

Explain to the children that they are going to make some plates of food for the self-service restaurant that you intend to set up in the classroom. Show them an apple. Ask them if an apple is a healthy food item. Can they tell you why? Draw out that it is healthy because it contains vitamins, no fat, natural sugar and so on. Show them the packet of crisps. Ask them if the crisps are healthy food items. Can they tell you why? Again, draw out that they are healthy because they contain some protein and no sugar, but unhealthy because they contain a lot of fat. Explain that they

contain fat because of the way they are cooked. The way food is cooked can make the food less healthy. You may like to explain at this point that all foods can be eaten, but some types of food, such as fat and sugar, should be eaten in smaller quantities. Show them the cream cake. Ask them whether the cream cake is a healthy food item. Can they tell you why? Elicit the fact that it is less healthy because it contains lots of fat and sugar and very few vitamins. Show the children the pictures of food that you have gathered together. Explain that they are going to make three food plates: a healthy food plate containing foods that they can eat lots of; a second food plate containing foods that they can eat a little of; and a third plate consisting of foods which they can eat occasionally but not too often. Spend a few moments discussing the foods in the pictures. On which plate, for example, would they put chips, peas, fish and sausages? Where would they put ice-cream, chocolate cake, yoghurt, oranges? Arrange the children into small groups and set them to work making the food plates. The groups will require continual input from yourself or another adult to reinforce the learning objective and reasons as to why certain foods are healthy or less healthy.

The children may wish to make food plates using plastic foods that are available in school or brought from home. They can also make posters for the restaurant showing the healthy food plates on one poster and the less healthy food plates on another. They may wish to make the less healthy food plates more expensive so that the healthiest plates are the cheapest and the unhealthiest plates are the most expensive.

## Suggestion(s) for extension

The more able children can plan and organize a 'Healthy eating' party where the guests will eat only healthy foods. Less healthy foods are banned! Invitations should reflect

the healthy eating concept. The children may also wish to plan and set up a healthy eating tuck shop which sells only healthy items such as fruit and vegetables.

## Suggestion(s) for support
Less able children may also like to plan and organize a healthy eating party. This would require additional adult support to discuss the issues.

## Assessment opportunities
Make a note of those children who can correctly choose a healthy food plate from the restaurant and thus understand the issues.

## Opportunities for IT
A simple clipart package can be used to import pictures of food items onto a circular design using a Draw program. The healthy food plates can be saved and printed, and incorporated into posters for the restaurant.

## Display ideas
Set up a self-service restaurant for the children's role-play. Customers to the self-service restaurant should be encouraged to choose the healthy eating plates of food and drinks. The healthey food plates can be saved and

## Other aspects of the Science PoS covered
Experimental and Investigative Science 3f. Section 0 2b.

## LEAVES
*Living things can be grouped according to similarities and differences.*
†† *Group activity.*
🕐 *30 minutes.*
⚠ *Safety: Collect leaves that are free from soil and other messy additions!*

### Previous skills/knowledge needed
It would be useful if the children had completed simple sorting activities such as the activity 'Soils' on page 47 in this book or 'Knock — on wood' on page 48 of *Curriculum Bank Science, Key Stage One*.

### Preparation
Make a survey of the area in which you intend to collect the leaves to ensure that it is safe and that there is a wide enough variety to carry out the activity. Make copies of photocopiable page 105 for those children carrying out the support activity.

### Key background information
This activity can be carried out at any time of the year, as all seasons will provide possibilities for comparison.

### Resources needed
A collection of leaves, blank labels and/or paper arrows, felt tipped pens. For the support activity – sorting rings, photocopiable page 105.

### Language to be introduced
Serrated, veins, leaflets, leaves, front, back, stalk, smooth, shiny, rough, dull.

### What to do
Go out with the children into the environment to collect leaves. Take them to an area close to the school where you know you will find a variety of leaves of different colours, sizes and shapes. On returning to the classroom, give the children the opportunity to handle the leaves. Encourage them to compare the sizes by placing one leaf next to or on top of another. Do their chosen leaves cover their hand, a two pence piece and so on? Ask them to sort all the leaves that are yellow, green, brown, red (if it is autumn), or different shades of green (if it is summer) and so on. Can they find all the leaves which have five points, red veins, prickly edges and so on? Ask a child to choose one leaf. What can the children tell you about it? Encourage them to describe its shape, size, colour and texture. Ask them to find another leaf which has something about it which is the same as the first leaf.

Arrange the children into a circle and invite them, one at a time, to show the rest of the class the leaf they have chosen and to say what feature of it is the same as the first leaf. Is it from the same variety of tree, the same colour, size, shape, texture? Repeat this activity until you are happy that the children are able to identify similarities.

Next, ask one child to choose another leaf. What can the children tell you about this leaf? This time, invite them each to find a leaf which is different in some way from the first leaf. Go around the circle and ask each child to say why they have chosen their particular leaf. What is different about their leaf? The children can display the leaves on a wall or board, linking them with arrows on to which they can write the similarities and differences they have observed.

### Suggestion(s) for extension

Use one type of leaf from the same species of tree. Record the similarities and differences using a Carroll diagram which allows the children to record same and different criteria.

|  | GREEN | NOT GREEN |
|---|---|---|
| WILL COVER A 2p COIN |  |  |
| WILL NOT COVER A 2p COIN |  |  |

If leaves from different species of tree are used, some children will be able to develop their thinking by suggesting unobservable similarities and differences such as the variety of tree the leaf comes from for example.

### Suggestion(s) for support

Once the children are able to identify simple similarities and common attributes, ask them to sort leaves which

are different in some way into sets using sorting rings. (You may need an additional adult to help here.) Limit the sorting to 'same' and 'different' criteria, for example prickly and not prickly. These can be recorded using photocopiable page 105. The adult can record the name of the sorting criteria, for example red/not red, yellow/not yellow, round/not round, pointed/not pointed, on to labels for the children to copy.

### Assessment opportunities

Make a note of which children are able to sort the leaves using simple criteria.

### Display ideas

Make large cut-outs of tree trunks and branches and display these to create a 3D effect. The sorted leaves can be painted with white PVA glue to preserve them and stuck to a tree cut-out to represent the chosen sorting criteria. This collage can act as a backcloth to children's written and other recorded work.

### Other aspects of the Science PoS covered

Experimental and Investigative Science 2a, 2b, 2c, 3c. Section 0 2c.

### Reference to photocopiable sheet

Photocopiable page 105 is a simple recording sheet onto which the children can draw the sorted leaves. Photocopy one sheet and enter the sorting label(s) before making the number of copies you need.

# MUNG BEANS

*Plants need water and light to become fully grown.*

♥♥ *Class or group activity.*

🕐 *60 minutes over a series of lessons.*

⚠ *Ensure that none of the children have an allergy to beansprouts.*

## Previous skills/knowledge needed

It would be useful if the children had looked closely at a variety of seeds and discussed their properties. You may like to look at the activity 'Sorting seeds' on page 32 of *Curriculum Bank Science, Key Stage One.* In this activity the children learn that seeds have observable similarities and differences.

## Preparation

Soak the mung beans overnight before you intend to plant them. Leave some mung beans unsoaked.

## Resources needed

Mung beans, trays, kitchen roll, water, cling film, black paper, beansprouts, paper, writing and drawing materials.

## Language to be introduced

Seeds, light, water, seed tray, spindly, leaves, stalk, sprout, dark, germination.

## What to do

Gather the children together so that they can all see the beansprouts. Show the children the beansprouts and explain that they are often used in Chinese cookery. Let the children try them. Next, show the children the mung bean seeds. Ask them what they notice about the colour, shape and size. Do they notice, for instance, that the seeds are spherical rather than flat, bigger than a cress seed but smaller than a bean seed?

Once the children have talked about the observable features, tell them that they are going to plant three lots of seeds. One batch will receive light but no water; the second batch will receive water but no light; and the final batch of seeds will receive both light and water. Explain that you want to show them that plants need water and light to grow. When the seeds have grown into plants, the class will compare them and note the similarities and differences.

Place some layers of kitchen roll into the three seed trays and scatter the

seeds which have been soaked overnight onto two of the trays. On the third tray, scatter seeds which have not been soaked overnight and explain to the children that this is the tray of seeds which will receive light but not water. Ask them at this point whether they think the seeds will grow. Can they give reasons for their opinions? Give the other two trays enough water to be absorbed into the kitchen towel so that when you press the towel, water seeps out. Cover all three trays with cling film, explaining to the children that this will help keep any warmth and moisture in the trays. Cover one of the trays containing the soaked seeds with several layers of black paper explaining to the children that this is to keep out the light. These are the seeds which will receive water but no light. Put the other two seed trays in a light place.

Remind the children that there are three seed trays.

▲ One tray contains seeds which will receive light but not water.

▲ One tray contains seeds which will receive water but not light.

▲ One tray contains seeds which will receive both light and water.

It is a good idea to label the trays accordingly because the children often forget which is which. After eight to ten days, remove the trays of seeds from their places. First, look at the seeds which received light but no water. What do the children notice? Can they tell you that the seeds did not grow because they did not get any water? Next, show them the seeds which received water but no light. What do they notice? They may notice that the plants look like the beansprouts at the beginning of the lesson. Encourage them to comment on the colour of the stems and leaves. Why do they think the beansprouts look spindly? Explain that they look like this because the plants

were looking for light. Finally, look at the seeds which received both water and light. The children should notice the dramatic difference between these plants and the ones which received no light. Make a list or draw the similarities

between the two sets of plantlets. They have both germinated (meaning the seeds have started to grow), they both have two leaves and a stem, and so on. Encourage the children to observe as many similarities as they can. Next, list all the differences between the two sets of plantlets. For instance, one is very green and the other is very pale yellow in colour. Stress to the children that the healthiest looking plantlets are the ones that received both light and water and that all plants need light and water to grow. The children can record the similarities and differences by drawing the two sets of plants.

### Suggestion(s) for extension

Carry out an investigation to demonstrate that other seeds do not need soil to grow but they do need water and light. Leave the plants for a longer period in the light and dark places and water them as appropriate. Is there a more dramatic difference after two weeks? Ask the children to make a note of the similarities and differences and to compare the two sets of results.

### Suggestion(s) for support

Less able children may need this concept reinforced. This could be achieved by repeating the experiment with cress seeds which grow very quickly. The children can then compare the results. They should notice that the cress left in the dark is a yellowy colour and very spindly; the cress left in the light and watered is very green; and the cress which received light but no water did not sprout or germinate.

### Assessment opportunities

Which children are able to conclude that the green plantlets are green because they received light, and therefore light allows plants to turn green? Make a note of the children who know that plants need both water and light to grow. Which children can design their own investigation using a different seed?

### Display ideas

Display the growth record of a plant. Start with a picture of a seed on the left of the display board; next display a picture of a seed which has just germinated; next to that display a picture of a plantlet; and finally display a picture of a plant. The fully grown plant can be labelled with the names of its parts. Suspend a watering can above the picture with droplets of water made from balls of cellophane falling from its spout and finally make a collage of the sun with rays of sunlight coming towards the plants. Label the water and light boldly. You may wish to make up a wall story entitled 'Jack and the mung bean!'.

### Other aspects of the Science PoS covered

Experimental and Investigative Science 2b, 2c, 3a, 3b, 3c, 3d. Section 0 1a, 1b, 2c, 3a, 4a, 4b.

# PUMPKINS

***Seeds grow into plants and plants grow.***

†† *Class or group activity.*

🕐 *60 minutes spread over several lessons.*

⚠ *Safety: Warn the children not to put seeds into ears, noses or mouths. Use seeds which have not been dressed with insecticide. It is always best to use compost bought from a reputable outlet or make sure that the compost you use has broken down fully and is free from additives! Ensure that the children keep hands away from mouths and make sure they wash their hands thoroughly at the end of the activity.*

## Previous skills/knowledge needed

It would be useful if the children knew that plants need light and water to grow (see the activity 'Mung beans' on page 33).

## Preparation

Make sure the compost is damp and safe for the children to handle.

## Key background information

The best time for planting to get an autumn crop is at the beginning of the summer term, ready to plant out during the second half of the term. The plants will need to be watered over the summer holiday by a reliable adult and the pumpkins should start to appear at the beginning of September. Use large pots in which to plant the seeds to prevent having to move the plantlets into larger pots. You may wish to grow some plants at home. These can be transported to school at the end of the summer holiday should the children's plants meet with disaster. It is likely that the children will have moved into new classes when you return to school after the summer holiday. If necessary you may have to work with another member of staff for the activity to be continued. Make copies of photocopiable page 106, one for each child.

## Resources needed

Large pots, compost, pumpkin seeds, grow bags or small area of garden, photocopiable page 106, drawing materials.

## Language to be introduced

Seeds, pots, compost, grow, plant, light, water, pumpkin, plantlet.

## What to do

Show the children a picture of a pumpkin or, if possible, remind them of the previous autumn when you may have made pumpkin lanterns as part of a study of Hallowe'en. Tell them that you are going to grow pumpkins for this autumn so that they can make Hallowe'en lanterns again.

Show the children the pumpkin seeds. Pass them around so that each child in the class handles one. What can they tell you about the size, shape and colour of the seed? Is the seed the same colour as the pumpkin? Can they give you reasons why not? Does the seed have a scent?

Explain that the children are going to plant two seeds in each pot. This is in case one of the seeds does not grow. Remind them how to plant the seeds. If you have previously carried out the activity 'Mung beans' on page 33, ask the children whether they can remember which conditions are necessary for seeds to grow. At this point demonstrate the planting procedure for the children to follow. (The children will be working individually within small groups of six to eight.) Once the children have planted their seeds, they should then find a good place to put their pots so that when the seeds begin to shoot, they will receive enough light. Explain why the pot should not be in direct sunlight (the soil or compost will dry out too quickly). The children may wish to write their name on a sticky label to put on their pot, or alternatively on a wooden, flat lollipop stick which can be pushed into the compost. Young children often forget which pot is theirs!

Once the plantlets have started to shoot, gather the children together to discuss what they can see. Have both seeds grown? Are they both the same size or is one taller than the other? How many leaves are on each plantlet?

Are they the same colour, shape and size? List the similarities and differences between the two plantlets. Next, give each child a copy of photocopiable page 106 and explain that they should use this to draw how the different plantlets look. Stress that their drawings must be as accurate as possible.

Towards the end of the first half of the summer term or shortly after the start of the second half of the summer term, the plantlets will be ready to plant out into a garden or growbag, whichever is appropriate to your school. Explain to the children that it is necessary to move the plantlets into a larger space as they need room to grow. If they do not have room, they will not grow large enough to produce the pumpkins. Encourage the children to plant out only the strong plants at this point to avoid any disappointment of some plants not growing. Also, the fully grown plants will need a lot of space. Only plant one plant in each growbag or one plant in each 60cm × 60cm square of garden.

Each child should complete a recording sheet. Encourage them to keep a note of the number and size of the leaves. Do the leaves stay the same size or do they grow? How do they know? Can they think of a way to measure the size of the leaves and the plant? Very young children can make comparative measurements. For example, 'On Monday the leaf was as big as my hand. On the following Monday the same leaf was as big as two hands', and so on.

One group may like to measure the size of the leaves and then cut out paper templates the same size. These can then be displayed and compared over the weeks. Explain the importance of watering the plants, particularly over the summer holiday. The plant should be mounded up so that when it is watered, it will not become waterlogged. A moat can be dug around the plant and filled with water so that the plant is not watered directly. Similarly, a tomato feed added to the water will help the pumpkins to grow. Follow the instructions on the label.

At the beginning of the autumn term, look carefully at the plants and discuss and record the differences between the plants since the end of July. Can they see a flower?

Are the pumpkins beginning to form on any of the plants? Are they able to see the pumpkin forming at the base of the flower? When the pumpkins are large enough, harvest one or two and cut them open. The children will be able to see the seeds easily and these can be discussed again. Do the children think that if you plant these seeds that a new pumpkin plant will grow. You could plant some and see.

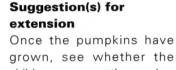

### Suggestion(s) for extension

Once the pumpkins have grown, see whether the children can count the number of seeds in their pumpkin. Are the number of seeds the same or different? Does the biggest pumpkin have the greatest number of seeds? The more able children will be able to record their findings on a bar chart.

### Suggestion(s) for support

You may find that very young or less able children will not have the patience to wait for pumpkins to grow. The same learning objective can be achieved through the growing of courgettes and marrows which, if planted under glass, can be harvested in July, thus enabling the activity to be completed before the holiday.

### Assessment opportunities

Make a note of those children who can predict that the seeds will grow into plants, and that the plants will grow and produce pumpkins. Which children are able to suggest that if they plant the seeds found inside the pumpkin they will grow into a new plant which will in turn yield more pumpkins and so on?

### Opportunities for IT

The children can use a simple graphing package to record the number of seeds found in each of the pumpkins. A record of growth can be made using a digital camera.

### Display ideas

The templates of the leaves can be displayed as a plant to show the weekly growth. The pictures can remain to form the backcloth for a display of Hallowe'en lanterns in the autumn term.

## Other aspects of the Science PoS covered

Experimental and Investigative Science 2a, 2b, 2c, 3a, 3b, 3c, 3d, 3e, 3f. Section 0 4a, 4b.

## Reference to photocopiable sheet

Photocopiable page 106 shows an illustration of two small stems. The children should complete the illustration, drawing their plantlets as accurately as possible and recording any similarities or differences.

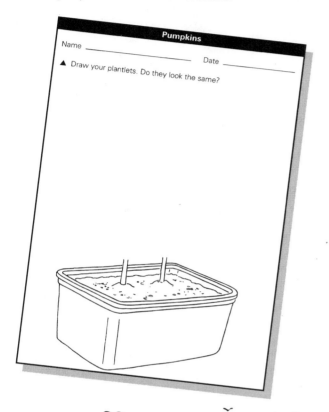

## ONE POTATO, TWO POTATOES

*To make careful observations, notice change and record findings in an investigation about potatoes.*

†† *Class or group activity.*

⏱ *60 minutes over a series of lessons.*

⚠ *Safety: Green potatoes are poisonous. Do not let the children eat them.*

## Previous skills/knowledge needed

You may wish to do this activity following the growing of potatoes.

## Preparation

Cut the storage label from a bag of potatoes which says 'Potatoes should be stored in a dry, dark, cool, frost-free place'. Investigate places to satisfy the required conditions. Find a potato which is beginning to go soft and starting to grow. Make copies of photocopiable page 107, one for each child.

## Resources needed

At least ten potatoes one of which should be soft and starting to grow, a frosty place (a freezer), a wet place (a polythene bag with water), a light place (a window-sill), a warm place (near a radiator) and a dry, dark, cool, frost-free place (outside shed or similar), a container, photocopiable page 107, writing and drawing materials.

## Language to be introduced

Frost, cool, dry, damp, warm, wet, dark, suitable.

## What to do

With the class, sing the song 'One potato, two potatoes' and talk about how potatoes grow under the ground and need to be stored properly once they have been dug up. Show the children the instructions on how to store potatoes. Ask them why they think it says the potatoes should be stored in a dry, dark, cool, frost-free place. Hopefully, some children will be able to tell you that it is to keep the potatoes from going rotten or to keep them fresh. Prompt them if they appear to be struggling.

Show the children a potato which has started to grow or go soft. Pass it around so that the children can feel it. Explain that this is happening because it has not been stored in a suitable place to keep it fresh. Next, explain that you are going to set up a test to find out what will happen if potatoes are not stored in a dry, dark, cool, frost-free place. What do they think will happen if they are stored in wet, light, warm or frosty places? It may be necessary to talk briefly about opposites here. Ask the children if they can think of a place which is not dry but is wet? Many children will suggest a container with water. Invite a child to put one potato into a container and cover it with water. Now ask them if they can think of a place which is not dark? Most children will suggest a window-sill or a place onto which the sun shines. Give a potato to another child and ask him or her to put it in the place that has been suggested. Next ask the children if they can think of a place which is not cool but warm. Children will probably suggest a radiator or heater. Invite a child to put the potato in the place suggested. (Make sure it is not a convector heater which should not have a grill obstructed or covered.) Next ask the children to think of a frosty place. The freezer compartment of a refrigerator is ideal. Finally, tell them

that it is important to put one potato in a dry, dark, cool, frost-free place as they are testing whether this place is a better place in which to keep potatoes fresh. With the children, discuss the possibilities around the school or go on a dark place hunt. This can be good fun. An outside store or a dark cupboard in a cool corridor is ideal. Hand out copies of photocopiable page 107. The children can use this to draw where each of the potatoes were stored. Retain the photocopiable pages for the children to return to later in the investigation.

After a few days, gather the children together and explain that you are going to look at the potatoes to see whether they are still in good condition. Hand back their copies of photocopiable page 107 for them to record their findings. Show them the potato which has been left in the freezer and tell them that you are going to leave it on the side to look at last. First of all, look at the potato in the container of water. It should be very soggy, soft and smelly. The children should observe that the potato has gone or is beginning to go rotten. If it is not too rotten, pass it around so that they can feel how soft it has become. Next, look at the potato which has been left on the window-sill. There may not be a significant change in the potato at this stage and you may need to leave it a while longer. However, you may be fortunate and find that the potato is already going green. Stress to the children that green potatoes should **not** be eaten. Can they give you a reason therefore why potatoes should not be stored in a light place? Are they able to tell you that the light will make the potatoes unsuitable to eat.

The potato which has been kept warm should have gone soft and wrinkly. The potato is starting to grow. The potato from the freezer will be frozen to begin with but as it defrosts, it will become soft, black and soggy. Fetch the potato from the dry, dark, cool, frost-free place and put it next to the other potatoes. Make a note of the children's responses.

## Suggestion(s) for extension

The more able children may like to record the measurements of change in more sophisticated ways, for example by weighing the potatoes or measuring their circumference, before and after the investigation noting whether any change in size has occurred.

## Suggestion(s) for support

Less able children may need to have discussed opposites in a previous lesson before being able to understand the opposite of dry, dark, cool and frost-free.

## Assessment opportunities

Make a note of which children are able to:

▲ make simple observations of what the potatoes look, feel and smell like;

▲ make more detailed observations of similarities and differences;

▲ notice the changes in the state of the potatoes;

▲ give simple explanations for the significance of the changes.

## Display ideas

Display pictures of large potatoes. Label them with the condition in which they were stored and a description of what happened to them. Cut out the heading MY POTATO WENT... in large letters and display above the pictures.

## Other aspects of the Science PoS covered

Life Processes and Living Things 3a. Section 0 1a, 1b, 2b.

## Reference to photocopiable sheets

Photocopiable page 107 provides spaces for the children to draw the places where the potatoes were stored and to record what happened to them.

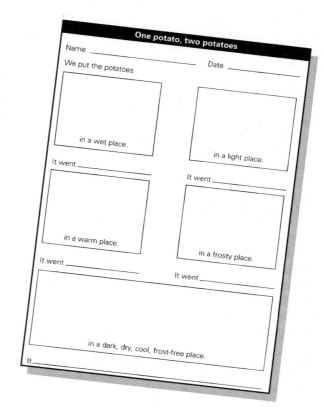

# MINIBEAST SAFARI

**Animals are all around us.**

†† *Class activity.*

🕐 *30 minutes.*

⚠ *Safety: Make sure that the children know not to handle any animals they find both for safety reasons and for the welfare of the animals themselves. Some children may have allergies which will need to be considered.*

## Previous skills/knowledge needed

The children should have completed a simple survey of animals which can be found in the school environment such as the activity on page 39 of *Curriculum Bank Science, Key Stage One* entitled 'Animals at school'.

## Preparation

Make a survey of the school grounds to ensure that they will provide enough minibeast life for the children to study. Look around the base and on the bark of trees for ants, under leaf litter for snails and woodlice, on the hedges and walls for spiders. If you have an area with long grass, you may find centipedes, worms and slugs. The week before you intend to go on the trail place logs, polythene sheeting, grass cuttings and leaf litter in a number of places in the school environment, for example in long grass, under hedges, under trees and so on. Empty, wet cardboard boxes are good for attracting snails and slugs, and sugar is good for attracting ants. An extra adult can be helpful for this activity. Make copies of photocopiable page 108, one for each child.

## Resources needed

Clipboards, pencils, polythene sheeting, logs, cardboard boxes, photocopiable page 108, writing materials. For the extension activity – reference materials on minibeasts.

## Language to be introduced

Names of any minibeasts you find. Small, under, damp, dry, habitat, environment, group, single.

## What to do

Explain to the children that they are going to go out into the school grounds to look for different kinds of very small creatures or minibeasts. They are going on a minibeast safari. Explain that a safari is when people go out to watch or observe animals in their natural habitat or environment. The children should be very careful not to disturb the animals or their habitat. They must only look and not touch! (You may wish to read them the poem by Christina Rosetti entitled 'Hurt no living thing'.)

Give each child a copy of photocopiable page 108. Tell them they must look carefully at the different minibeasts they see in the various places and then draw them in the appropriate section on the photocopiable sheet. Alternatively, they could use the sheet to note down observations about the minibeasts they see in the different areas. Take the children into the school grounds and go to the first observation point. Look around the chosen place, being careful if you move any logs, leaf litter, and so on to reinstate the habitat as closely as possible to its natural state. Talk to the children about the creatures they can see. Ask questions such as:

▲ *Is there more than one of the same kind of creature?* Ants, for example, live in colonies and if you can see one there is always another not too far away.

▲ *Is the area damp or dry?*

▲ *What is the habitat like? Is it sheltered, in long grass, under something?*

▲ *How big is the creature? Is it bigger than the nail on your little finger?*

▲ *Has the creature legs?* Can the children count how many or is the creature moving too fast to be able to count?

Visit all of the areas in the school grounds where you know there to be small creatures. You may be lucky to see insects such as ladybirds, butterflies, wasps and bees during the summer or early autumn months.

On returning to the classroom, allow the children to draw or paint the animals of their choice.

## Suggestion(s) for extension

Explain to the children that you are going to collect a few of the creatures in magnispectors and on return to the classroom look carefully at each one. Explain the need for care, that they must only look not touch and that the minibeasts will be returned to where they were found as quickly as possible so as not to cause distress. Invite each child to look carefully and to notice something different about the creature – possibly its size, the number of legs, the way it moves, body segments or features such as mouth, eyes and hair. If you have gathered any reference materials, allow the children to research life cycles and other information about the minibeasts they have observed.

## Suggestion(s) for support

Some children will need to work as part of a very small group with adult help so that their attention can be kept focused on the observation of the creatures. Prompt sheets with appropriate questions for the adult to ask would ensure the learning objective is clearly focused. Also, instead of using the photocopiable sheet during the activity, they can be helped to collate the information they have found about the creatures on to it afterwards.

## Assessment opportunities

Some children will be able to tell you the names of the creatures and the animal group they belong to. Some may even be able to give reasons as to why certain creatures were found where they were.

## Opportunities for IT

There are some good commercial multimedia CDs available. If you have or are able to obtain any of these, the children can use them to find out more about the creatures they have found. If you are lucky enough to be connected to the Internet, you may find a suitable website onto which you can contribute the children's survey and find out more about minibeasts in different environments and habitats around the world.

## Display ideas

There are many creative ways that the childen's paintings can be displayed. Alternatively make a collage of long grass and leaves which can be extended onto a table-top to create a 3D effect. Suspend models of minibeasts that the children have made from junk materials around the collage and place other models and cut-out pictures into the leaf and grass background. Printed out pictures obtained from the IT package could also be incorporated.

## Other aspects of the Science PoS covered

Experimental and Investigative Science 2a, 2b, 2c, 3a, 3b. Section 0 1b, 1c, 1d, 2a, 2c, 4a, 4b, 5a.

## Reference to photocopiable sheet

Photocopiable page 108 contains pictures of the habitats you are likely to visit. The children can draw the minibeasts they see next to the appropriate habitat and write down any brief notes or comments.

# BIRDS

*Different species of the same animal sometimes visit the same habitat.*

†† *Class observation.*

🕐 *Introductory lesson 45 minutes and then 15 minutes on a daily basis over a short period of time.*

⚠ *Safety: Clear away any food scraps left outside after the activity to discourage rats and other wildlife which it may attract. Be aware of the health and hygiene implications of handling and storing food in the classroom. Bird food will attract rodents and should be stored in rodent-proof containers.*

## Previous skills/knowledge needed

The children should have carried out the activity 'Minibeast safari', see page 40 which looks at different species of small animals who share the same habitats.

## Key background information

Remind the children of the moral issues surrounding the investigation of wildlife and that it is not acceptable to experiment on the natural world in a thoughtless way. It is very important that the birds do not come to rely on the food left out, therefore the activity should curtail after a short period of time. It is best to do this activity before young birds leave their nest as they need to learn to find natural food for themselves in the environment.

## Preparation

If birds are not already visiting your playground, following morning or lunchtime play, make sure there are a few crumbs of tuck or lunch left for the birds to feed on. Alternatively, you could leave a small amount of shop-bought bird food outside or make feeders such as those in the activity 'Birds' on page 93 of Curriculum Bank Science, Key Stage One. Sometimes, after a few days, the birds will start to visit the playground regularly in order to feed on any scraps. (You may find out that this takes longer in some areas due to other factors such as the number of predators, noise and birds such as crows and magpies.) You may like to make a note of the species so that you can add these to the photocopiable sheet before photocopying. Set up a place where the children can observe the birds without disturbing them, as birds are easily frightened off. A classroom window facing the playground would be a good place, and it may be necessary to swap classrooms with a colleague for a session. Make copies of photocopiable page 109, one for each child. Make an enlarged copy for demonstration with the class.

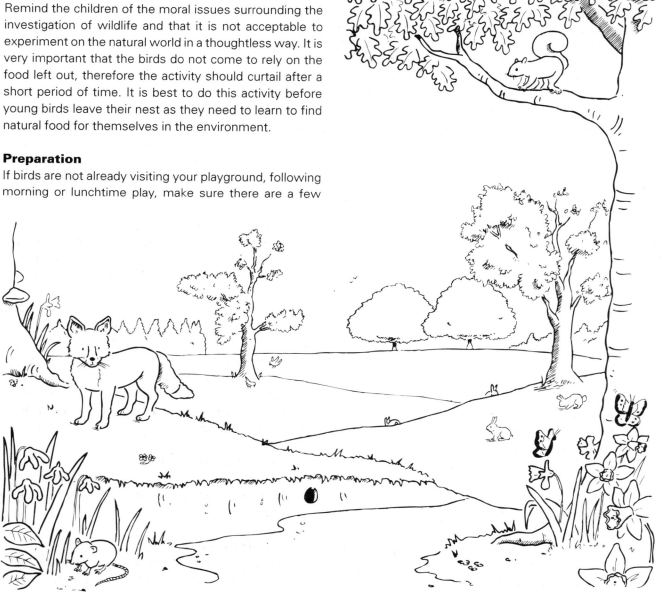

**Resources needed**
Small scraps of food or bird food, photocopiable page 109, writing materials, reference books for the identification of birds.

**Language to be introduced**
Birds, species, wildlife.

**What to do**
Before morning or lunchtime play on the first occasion that you intend to carry out the observations, gather the children together to explain what they are going to do. Tell them that they are going to make a survey of the different kinds of birds that visit the playground, and that you have decided to do this after morning and lunchtime play every day. Discuss with them the procedures for observation, such as the need to keep very quiet, not to make any sudden noises and so on. Explain that today you are going to make the observations together so that everyone will know what they have to do. However, from tomorrow they are going to take it in turns to collect the information. With the class, look at your enlarged copy of photocopiable page 109. The children can use individual copies of the photocopiable sheet to record the different birds by naming, drawing or completing a tick or tally chart, or you may wish to complete one class sheet together. Alternatively, as mentioned in 'Preparation', you may wish to add the names of the birds you are likely to see first before photocopying it for the children to use as a tick or tally chart.

Take the children to the observation spot and observe the numbers of birds in the playground. How many birds are there? Are the birds of the same or different species? How do they know? Discuss the colour, size and features of the birds. Are they the same in any way? Are there any differences? Emphasize that they are all birds, but that they are different species.

On returning to the classroom, discuss the information gathered. How many kinds of birds visited the playground? How many of the same kind visited? Was there one kind of which there were more visitors than another? Can the children give reasons why? Spend about two weeks collecting information in this way until you have a list of the different varieties of birds which have visited the playground. Were there any other visitors? Depending on where your school is, you may find that there were a few squirrels for instance. Now is the time to collate all the information you have collected about the animals you have found in the school environment from both this and  other activities. Stick pictures of all the different kinds of animals you have found on a

large sheet of paper to display on the wall. Draw the children's attention to the number you have found and explain that lots of different kinds of animals can be found in the same environment. The activity can be repeated in different environments, for instance a local park, farm or woodland.

**Suggestion(s) for extension**
The more able children can analyse the information in greater detail. The activity can be repeated at different times of the day or year, or at different places to compare the number and different kinds of visitor. Are visitors more likely to come at certain times or places? Do some environments have certain birds and not others?

**Suggestion(s) for support**
Another adult will be required to support the groups during their observations and help the children to record the information accurately. If an additional adult is not available, it may be wise to carry out the survey as a class activity.

**Assessment opportunities**
Which children know that different animals are found in the same environment and can give reasons for their knowledge?

**Opportunities for IT**
Children can access a CD to identify different kinds of birds. You may wish to surf the Internet to see if other

schools are doing a similar activity in order to compare information. It would be particularly useful if a school in a very different environment were doing the same type of survey as you may find they have collected very different, or perhaps more interestingly, very similar results. For instance, you could compare the similarities and differences between rural and inner city schools; European and Asian schools; schools near the coast and those inland.

### Display ideas
Make a giant picture of all the animals found in the school environment and display it in a semi-permanent place where the children can continue to add pictures of animals as they are observed over a period of time. It may be appropriate to carry out this activity over a whole year so that seasonal differences can be discussed.

### Other aspects of the Science PoS covered
Experimental and Investigative Science 1a, 1b, 1c, 2a, 2b, 2c, 3a, 3b, 3c, 3d, 3e, 3f. Section 0 1a, 1b, 1c, 2a, 2c, 4b, 5a, 5b.

### Reference to photocopiable sheet
Photocopiable page 109 is a recording sheet on which the children can record the different types of birds that they see in their school environment. The children can draw or write the names of the birds as well as noting down any comments or observations.

# WRIGGLING WORMS

*Animals move, feed and grow.*

**†† ** *Class activity.*

**🕐 ** *45 minutes.*

**⚠ ** *Safety: An additional adult to support the collection of worms would be useful for animal welfare and health and safety reasons. Remind the children of the importance of washing hands after handling foliage or animals, this includes worms. They could wear very small disposable gloves like those used for First Aid.*

### Preparation
Make or acquire a wormery or use a plastic sweet jar. You will need a variety of different types of coloured soils. To make a wormery you will need three pieces of wood: one piece approximately 30cm × 1cm × 3cm and two pieces 20cm × 1cm × 3cm; and two pieces of perspex 20cm × 30cm. Fix the wood together to make a frame and then fix the two pieces of perspex to each side of the frame. Fill the wormery to about ten centimetres from the top with layers of different kinds and coloured soils. Make copies of photocopiable page 110, one for each child.

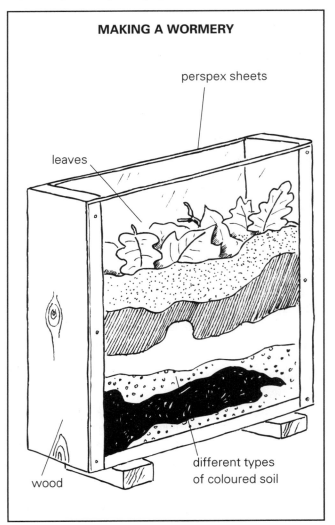

**MAKING A WORMERY**

perspex sheets

leaves

wood

different types of coloured soil

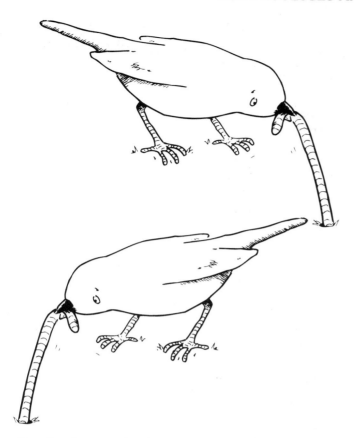

### Key background information

You may wish to collect the worms yourself. The best time of year to find worms is in the autumn especially under leaf litter, although they have been found on the playground on a damp spring morning. The worms should be picked up cleanly, between first finger and thumb, taking care not to rub them across the surface they are found on. Scraping across the ground can cause extreme damage and considerable stress to the worm. It is important to remember that worms cannot survive in very hot or very dry conditions so the wormery should be kept damp and displayed away from heat sources such as radiators and the sun. At the end of the activity, all worms should be returned to their natural habitat and, if possible, to the site from which they were collected.

### Resources needed

A wormery, a variety of different kinds and coloured soils (chalk, lime, sand, compost are good) placed in the wormery in layers, black sugar paper, plastic containers, magnifying lens, leaves, different kinds of fruit and vegetables, photocopiable page 110. For the support activity – a class visitor.

### Language to be introduced

Stretch, segments, tail, head, move, grow, wormery, sand, compost, soil.

### What to do

Take the children out into the immediate environment on a damp morning or after a wet warm night and collect some worms. You should be able to find plenty of these in the playground or field. If you are unable to see any worms, look for signs on the field such as worm castes or small holes and dig a small area around these. Carefully pull the grass apart to find the worms inside. Put the collected worms very carefully into a plastic container. Place one worm on a damp sheet of perspex; this will allow the children to observe the movements of the worm. Explain to the children the importance of treating all living things with respect and care, and that they must not put the worm under any stress. Tell the children that worms cannot survive in very hot or very dry conditions. You may wish to wait until you have returned to the classroom before explaining this.

On returning to the classroom, ask the children what they notice about the size, shape and colour of the worm. Allow one child to use a magnifying lens to observe the worm. What can the child see? Can he or she see any arms and legs? A mouth, nose, ears or eyes? Can the child tell which end is the head and which is the tail? This may be a good time to tell the children that if the worm is accidentally chopped in half, the front half will eventually grow a new tail! Emphasize why you are not going to test this theory! Explain how the worm is made up of a number of body segments. Do they notice anything else? They may be able to see tiny hairs along the length of the body, or the saddle.

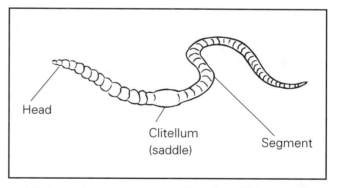

Head

Clitellum (saddle)

Segment

Ask how the worm moves. Can the children think of another animal which moves in the same way? Stress the fact that all animals move. Are all worms the same size? Are some bigger than others? Can the children give you a reason why some worms are bigger. With the class, reach the conclusion that all animals grow and because worms are animals they too grow.

Talk to the children about the wormery you have made or acquired. Explain that the wormery will make a good temporary home for the worms but that they will have to be returned very carefully to their natural homes in a few weeks time. In the meantime the children must look after the worms very carefully and make sure they are well cared for in their classroom.

Tell the children that you have found a warm and dark place for the wormery to be kept – the same conditions

as under the ground – and that it is very important to keep the soil damp. (If appropriate, you may wish to explain the concept of damp at this point.) Place the worms carefully in the wormery and allow them to settle down. Explain to the children how important it is to let the worms settle and explore their new home. The wormery can become part of an interactive display where the children can observe how the worms mix up the soils. If you put black paper over the sides of the wormery, the darkness created will encourage the worms to come to the sides where the children will be able to observe their movements. Discourage the children from touching and trying to handle the worms. They will disturb the wormery if they do. Put different kinds of leaves, fruit and vegetables on top of the wormery and make a note of which foods the worms like best. Do they have a favourite? Give each child a copy of photocopiable page 110 on which to record the worms' food preferences.

## Suggestion(s) for extension

The more able children can research why gardeners like worms, who the worms natural enemies are and how worms survive in dry conditions. They can also make a simple bar chart of the foods the worms eat most. Cover one side of the wormery with black paper and leave the other side uncovered. The children can then compare the activity on the two sides of the wormery. Are the layers of soils mixed to the same extent? Is there a difference in the amount of activity?

## Suggestion(s) for support

Less able children may need more time to observe the worms in the wormery and to apply the new language they have learned. This can be done by inviting a visitor

into the classroom and then 'choosing' specific children to tell their visitor everything they have learned about worms. Ask the visitor to make a note of whether the children know that worms move, grow and feed.

## Assessment opportunities

A simple recording sheet will provide evidence of which children know worms move, grow and feed. If a class visitor does come and visit, make a note of which children are able to explain what they have learned and observed.

## Display ideas

Make a large 'under the ground' picture on a wall behind the table or surface where you intend to put the wormery. The picture can contain other creatures which live under the ground as well as root systems. Above the ground, display pictures of the worms' natural enemies, with the rules of how the worms should be cared for prominently displayed. A selection of hand magnifiers should be made available for the children's continuing observations.

## Other aspects of the Science PoS covered

Experimental and Investigative Science if you decide to plan an investigation into the difference between the two sides of the wormery. Section 0 1a, 1b, 1c, 2c, 4a, 4b, 5a, 5b.

## Reference to photocopiable sheet

Photocopiable page 110 is a recording sheet on which the children can record the worms' food preferences.

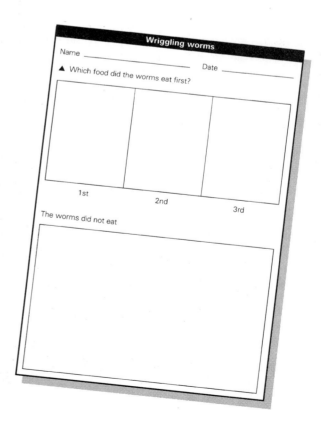

# Materials and their properties

This section of the book contains tried and tested teaching activities that have been shown to enhance children's knowledge and understanding of materials. The lessons make use of a wide range of readily available materials and engage the children in practical, investigative, science wherever possible.

Many of the lessons encourage the children to participate in the whole scientific process from initial observation through practical investigation to the communication of findings and results. Helpful suggestions for pupil and teacher recording of results are provided, as well as ideas for teacher assessment.

A full list of lessons is included in the overview grid on pages 7–11 at the beginning of this book.

## SOILS

***We use our senses to recognize the properties of certain materials.***

†† *Class activity organized into groups of 4 or 6.*

🕐 *45 minutes.*

⚠ *Safety: It would be best if you knew where the soils came from so that you could ensure they are safe for the children to handle. Also obtain some sand, gravel and compost. The children should not put their fingers into their mouths after handling the soils until they have washed their hands thoroughly in hot soapy water and used a nail brush to clean their nails. An extra adult to supervise this would be useful.*

### Preparation

Create a collection of different types of garden soil. Place the different soils into various containers – ice-cream containers are fine – enough for each group to have a set.

### Resources needed

Peat, compost, sand, clay, gravel, varieties of garden soil, ice-cream containers, sorting rings, labels, felt-tipped pens.

### Language to be introduced

Fine, dirty, compost, soil, sticky, clay, flows, sand, sandy, stones, gravel, peat, brown, black, texture, rough, smooth, gritty, soft, grain.

## What to do

Gather the children into a circle around the sorting rings (use up to four) and one of the set of soils. Explain to the children that they are going to find out about the soils using their senses of touch and sight. Pass the sand around the circle and ask the children to carefully feel its texture. Encourage them to describe what the sand feels like. Does it feel soft, rough, hard, gritty? Does it flow through their fingers or does it stick to them? Can they roll the sand into a ball? Are their hands clean or dirty? At this point explain the hygiene rules to the children and the importance of not putting their fingers into or near their mouths until they have been washed thoroughly using a nail brush and hot soapy water. Explain why. Pass the sand around again. Ask the children to smell the sand and to look at it very carefully. Can they describe what it looks like? Encourage them to describe the sand further, for instance its colour and smell.

Does it have a smell that they can describe in words or even by using an expression? 'Ugh' can often be used for sorting purposes! Ask the children to choose two attributes that they have suggested, for example 'brown' 'flowing', or 'rough' 'sticky'. Label the sorting rings with a single attribute.

Tell the children that you want them to look carefully and to feel and smell the other types of soil you have in the containers. Explain that you want them to sort them by placing them in the correct set. Repeat the activity with the other soils. It may be necessary to use different attributes chosen by the children. You may find that you can develop the activity by sorting using overlapping sets where some soils satisfy the criteria of both sets, for example the children may choose 'grey' and 'sticky' for their attributes in which case clay could meet both criteria. Are the children able to make up a name for the soil they are feeling, for example the soil that is both rough and flows through their fingers, or that is rough and has stones? After washing their hands the children can record their work using a simple Venn diagram.

## Suggestion(s) for extension

Some children will be able to sort the soils into 'same' and 'different' criteria using Carroll diagrams. For example, they can be sorted into brown/not brown, soft/not soft. Can they tell you the name of the soils which are brown and not soft? Other pairs of criteria could include 'brown and rough', 'grey and sticky', 'rough and with stones'. Can they tell you the name of the soils that are not rough and

do not have stones? Limit the collection to a variety of sands and repeat the activity with this much smaller range of soils.

## Suggestion(s) for support

Some children may benefit from the assistance of an additional adult and will need to be taught specific vocabulary to describe the soils.

## Assessment opportunities

Make a note of the children who use their senses to sort the soils into sets and who use appropriate language to support their choices.

## Opportunities for IT

A concept keyboard linked to a word processor can be used to record the children's work. The concept keyboard could have pictures of the various soils and a list of words which the children can match. For example the picture of sand could be linked to gritty, rough or brown giving a sentence on screen of 'The sand is gritty/rough/brown'.

## Display ideas

The soils can be used to fill a wormery for the activity 'Wriggling worms' on page 44 and can form part of the display suggestion in that activity.

## Other aspects of the Science PoS covered

Experimental and investigative Science 2a, 2b, 2c. Life Processes and Living Things 2f. Section 0 1b, 4a, 5a, 5b.

# POURING OIL OVER WATER

*To explore materials and objects using appropriate senses, making observations and communicating these.*

✝✝ *Whole class investigation followed by small group work.*

🕐 *30 minutes.*

⚠ *Safety: Make sure that the children are aware that oil does not come out of clothes easily. They should therefore wear aprons, preferably long-sleeved ones, in order to keep their clothes fully covered at all times. Have a supply of paper towels on which the children can wipe their hands before washing them. By the end of the lesson they should know that oil and water do not mix and that washing hands alone in water is a waste of time! Soap has to be used.*

*NB. Children should **not** handle the motor oil. Oil should also not be added to class water trays. Do not use aquaria or other containers which may subsequently be used for housing wildlife.*

## Previous skills/knowledge needed
Children will need to have had experience of seeing objects floating and sinking through directed play in the water tray.

## Key background information
In this lesson children explore the similarities and differences between solids and liquids.

## Preparation
Collect 'floaters and sinkers' from the water tray and have them to hand when you introduce this lesson. You will need to experiment a little for yourself if you have not tried these ideas already. The children will need to wear art aprons, and tables should be covered if you allow the children to carry out their own investigations. During the activity, each group will need a container filled with water.

## Resources needed
'Floaters and sinkers' such as corks, plastic containers, lightweight wooden bricks, a stone or brick, an apple, a coin, polystyrene ball and a toy car; a water tray (preferably one that is transparent so that the whole class will be able to see the floaters and sinkers clearly, or, alternatively, several smaller trays), water, cooking oil, motor oil, bowls/trays for water, pipettes/droppers for oil and, if required, oil-based paints for marbling, wooden stick, art aprons, paper towels, table covering. For the extension activity – screw-top jars.

## Language to be introduced
Float to the top, sink to the bottom, mix, mixed together, separated, solid, hard, liquid, runny, pour.

## What to do
Talk to the children about floating and sinking. Show them the collection of floaters and sinkers you have obtained and explain that they are going to sort them into sets according to whether they will float or sink. Show each object to the children and ask them to predict whether the object will float or sink. Explain to the children that the objects you have chosen are all solid objects, they can all be held in the hand and are not 'runny'. Test each one to discover what it does.

If you feel that the children would benefit by being challenged further you may like to introduce the idea of solids and liquids at this stage. Show them the motor oil and ask them whether they think it is a solid. The more able children will be able to compare the properties of the oil to the solid objects and give explanations as to how it is different. Reach the conclusion that oil is classified as a liquid because it is runny, can be poured and takes the shape of the container it is poured into. Solids are not runny and cannot be poured.

Tell the children they have now seen for themselves that some solid objects float and others sink. Explain that they are now going to investigate whether one liquid, oil, will float or sink. (Make sure all the other objects have been removed from the tray.) Show the children the motor oil and tell them that it is a liquid. Explain that you are

going to pour some of the oil into the water tray. Ask the children: Who thinks the oil will float? Who thinks it will sink? Take a show of hands and record the result. You can physically divide the class according to their voting pattern, or make a line of counters or cubes to represent the number of votes cast for each option.

Now pour a few droplets of motor oil into the tray and observe what happens. The children should notice that the oil floats on top of the water. Soak up the oil with a piece of absorbent paper; kitchen paper is ideal. Not only is this a good way to clear the oil, but the children will be fascinated by the process.

Repeat the activity, this time using cooking oil. How many children are able to use their previous knowledge to predict correctly that the oil will float? Once again show the children what happens and ask them to explain what they have observed. At this point, organize the children into small groups and give each group a container filled with water. Hand out the cooking oil and droppers. Spend a few moments explaining that in some ways oil behaves like some solids because it floats on top of the water. Ask the children in which set they would put the oil. Does it belong with the floaters or sinkers? Hopefully, most children will say that it should belong with the floaters! Tell the children to now add a few drops of cooking oil to the water. What does the oil do?

Reinforce the concept by adding some oil-based paint to water in a shallow tray large enough for a sheet of A4 absorbent paper to fit. Stir the water with a stick to make a pattern in the oil paint before placing the sheet of A4 paper on top. The children will notice that the oil paint is soaked up and the pattern is transferred to the paper. (This activity can be included in a series of group activities throughout the week as it is difficult to do marbling with large groups of children and will probably need to be done a few at a time unless you have considerable adult support.)

## Suggestion(s) for extension
Can the children make the oil sink? Give each group a jar half-filled with water. What do they think will happen when cooking oil is added to the water? Tell the children to add some oil and then shake the jars. If the oil becomes emulsified in the water then leave it to separate. How long does this take? Does it float to the top? Ask the children to develop their own investigation.

## Suggestion(s) for support
Children requiring support may need additional adult help to develop the concepts explored in this lesson. They will also benefit from additional time spent carrying out practical floating and sinking activities.

### Assessment opportunities
This lesson provides many opportunities for assessment of individuals through direct questioning. If you have an adult helper available, he or she could note down some of the children's responses for you.

### Display ideas
Display the children's marbling patterns with the words used to describe the solids and liquids. The sets of floaters and sinkers used at the beginning of the activity can be left on a table-top display for the children to add to during their continuing investigations. This could include other oils and liquids which can be added to water in transparent containers in order for the children to observe their behaviour.

### Other aspects of the Science PoS covered
Experimental and investigative Science lb, 2b, 3e, f. Section 0 1a, 1b, 3a, 4a, 5a, 5b.

# SORT OUT YOUR COLOUR TABLE

*To be able to sort objects into sets of common materials and to recognize some of the properties.*

†† *Whole class introduction followed by group activity.*

🕐 *30 minutes.*

⚠ *Safety: Take care to ensure that all the items brought into school for the display are suitable for your pupils to handle.*

## Previous skills/knowledge needed

Children will gain most benefit from this activity if they have had previous experience of sorting collections of materials for colour, shape and size.

## Preparation

Set aside a low display table on which to create your colour collection. Enlist the help of other adults and children in your class to bring in items for the collection. Choose a colour and explain that the items must all be in this colour. Try to include as wide a variety of materials in your collection as possible. Immediately before the lesson, jumble up the collection so that it looks as if someone has piled loads of things into a heap on the table.

## Resources needed

A collection of items in one colour but made from as wide a variety of materials as possible to form a colour table display, sorting rings/PE hoops (alternatively you could use pieces of sugar paper to act as sorting mats), notepad on which to record children's criteria for sorting, folded card strips, felt-tipped pen, blindfold (optional). For the extension activity – a small selection of information books, question or cloze procedure sheets.

## Language to be introduced

Sort, sets, materials, plastic, leather, wood, wooden, textiles, metal, paper.

## What to do

Sit the children in a circle around the collection so that they can all see and handle the items. Make sure there is enough room for the sorting rings to be laid out. Talk to the children about how the collection could be 'sorted out'. Tell them that the collection is important and that you want them to organize the objects into a display which will need to be kept sorted all the time. Try to draw out the children's own ideas for sorting and, when appropriate, introduce the criteria of 'materials' or 'what the objects are made of'.

Explore the children's knowledge of materials. Ask them what they can see. What can they tell you about the colour

of the objects? Explain that you have chosen the same colour because you want them to concentrate on the materials from which the objects are made. Ask whether there are any shiny objects, things in which they can see their reflection? Are there any transparent objects, things they can see through? Are there any dull objects? Pass the objects around and ask the children to say what each object feels like. Which objects are smooth, rough, hard, soft, and so on? Next, ask the children what they notice about the material from which the objects are made. Can they sort the set of wooden objects, the paper objects and so on? You will probably find that at the end of this sorting activity there will be a number of objects that the children are unsure of. Discuss their properties and tell the children from which material they are mostly made. (Many manufactured items are made from a combination of materials. You will need to select a 'best fit' set for each object.) Direct them to the set to which it belongs. Label the sets with the correct 'materials' name by writing something like 'All these things are made from wood' and so on.

Follow-up group activities will enable you to talk about each material in turn. Look closely at, for example, the objects made from wood. Are they all the same texture? Do they all look the same? Are the objects made from glass all transparent? Are the metals all reflective or are some dull?

You may like to transfer the sets to a display area. Once this has been done, you can play a game with the children by adding or moving things into the wrong sets when they are not looking. This game can develop over the course of a week so, for instance, after every playtime the children know that they have to look at the display and find the object or objects which you have moved or added, and put them back in their right places. Some children really enjoy the 'double bluff' element of this game as the teacher pretends not to know who is being 'naughty' and moving things around!

## Suggestion(s) for extension

Ask the children to make a collection of objects from the classroom. Introduce the concept of natural and man-made materials to this group. Using question sheets or cloze procedure sheets, encourage the children to use a small preselected set of information books to research these materials and their various sources or method of manufacture.

## Suggestion(s) for support

If children seem unable to move on from sorting for size and colour you may wish to spend some time working with attribute sets before returning to the activity described in this lesson. With sufficient experience of sorting, children should be able to go beyond colour, shape and size when sorting a collection.

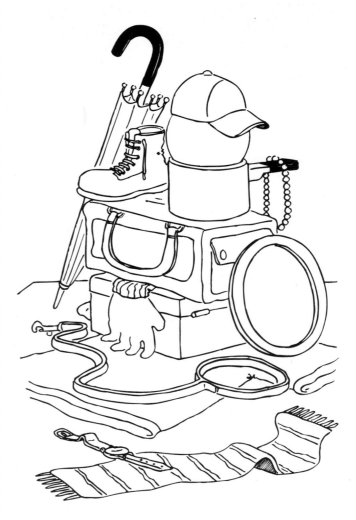

## Assessment opportunities

Make a note of those children who cannot progress beyond size and shape as criteria for sorting. Also watch for more able children who may attempt to create their own original criteria for sorting, such as 'things that are fun to play with/ things that are not good for playing with'.

## Opportunities for IT

Children can use a Micropedia or similar CD to research materials, their sources and method of manufacture.

## Display ideas

This activity lends itself very well to a display. The display can be enhanced if a backdrop of shiny, reflective materials is used and textile hangings added. Photographs of children creating the sets and carrying out related thematic work provide a good finishing touch, especially in the lead up to a parents evening!

## Other aspects of the Science PoS covered

Experimental and Investigative Science 2a 2b 2c. Section 0 1b, 1c, 1d, 4a.

# ROCK IN A SOCK

*We can use our sense of touch to explore a range of common materials and use our knowledge of properties to identify them.*

†† *Group activity.*

🕐 *30 minutes.*

⚠ *Safety: Make sure that the children are reminded about the hardness of some materials and the need to be very careful when handling the socks.*

## Previous skills/knowledge needed

The children will need to have handled and sorted a collection of materials before this lesson.

## Key background information

This activity can be turned into an on-going classroom task and can be included in many classroom themes. More able pupils can be encouraged to help you plan and run the activity for the rest of the class.

## Preparation

Collect an interesting range of materials; these should include wood, textiles, plastic, rock, paper and metal, as these are the main materials Key Stage One children should be able to identify. The collection could comprise raw materials, manufactured items, natural objects, items found in a certain area (for example the classroom or the kitchen) or it could be made up of a mixture of all these things. You will need several samples of each material which should be small enough to fit inside a sock.

Collect some socks. (Make sure the children cannot see through them.) Hang an improvised washing line in the classroom fairly low so that the children can add and remove items for themselves. Write some display labels for your collection.

## Resources needed

Collection of materials, socks, washing line (or string), clothes pegs which are not too strong for young fingers to operate, labels. A kick step could be helpful for some children.

## Language to be introduced

Rock, metal, wood, textiles, paper, plastic.Stretched, bent, squashed, twisted, hard, soft, springy, fluffy, rigid, flexible.

## What to do

Show the children your collection of materials and remind them that they have already seen and sorted a collection of objects in a previous lesson. Remind the children of the names of the materials and, if necessary, suggest some of the materials' characteristics which may help with

their identification. Can the material be stretched, bent, squashed, twisted? Is the material hard, soft, springy, fluffy, rigid, flexible? Show the children the socks and the washing line. Tell them that you are going to put one material in each sock and that you are going to hang the socks on the washing line. Very carefully, making sure that the children cannot see, place the materials in the socks. Hang the socks securely to the washing line.

Challenge the children to identify which material is in which sock by using their sense of touch and knowledge about each material's properties. Allow the children time to investigate but do not allow anyone to look inside the socks or to take them off the line.

When appropriate, gather the children together and record their predictions. Ask them how they came to their particular conclusion about the materials. Did they identify the wood correctly because it was hard and rigid, or did some children correctly identify the material because they recognized the object made from wood? If the children are struggling, direct their thinking by questioning them about the properties of the material. For example, ask them whether the material is squashy. If the answer is yes, explain that the material cannot be wood because wood is not squashy. Finally, allow the children to check whether their predictions were correct by removing the materials from the socks.

If the group carried out the activity successfully you may like them to repeat the task only this time using more difficult samples. If they found the exercise difficult you can use the same set of materials again, placing the objects in different socks and/or putting the socks in a different order. Alternatively, you could use two sets of identical materials, placing one sample into a sock and the other onto a table top for the children to refer to to help them identify the materials.

At the end of the group's time on this activity they can help you set up the socks for the next group. They may then wish to stay and watch while the new children try to name the materials.

Finally, ask the children to replace the materials back on the display table. Have your labels with the names of the materials ready to place.

## Suggestion(s) for extension

Extend the collection of materials to include sand, soil, leaves, dried rice or peas and vegetables.

## Suggestion(s) for support

Play 'Kim's game' using the materials from your collection to help reinforce the names of all the materials. Place one object made from each of the materials, the names of which you want the children to learn, on a tray. Spend a short time discussing and naming the materials. Explain to the children that when you ask them to close their eyes, you will remove one of the objects. When they open their eyes, they must say which material you have removed

from the tray. When you play the game some children will still say the name of the object. If they do say something like: *Well done. Yes it was the (toy car). What material was it made from?* This will continually keep the children thinking about the material even when naming the object.

## Assessment opportunities

Identify those children who are able and unable to identify or name the materials contained within the socks.

## Display ideas

The socks hanging on the washing line form a display in their own right. You may like to hang questions on the line to encourage the children to return to the activity. Have the collection of materials with the materials' names on a display table nearby.

## Other aspects of the Science PoS covered

Life Processes and Living Things 2f. Experimental and Investigative Science 2a. Section 0 1b, 4a.

# A PLASTIC WORLD

*Different everyday objects can be made from materials we call plastics.*

†† *Class introduction and group investigation.*

🕐 *40 minutes.*

⚠ *Safety: Remind the children of the dangers of suffocation from polythene bags and any other items associated with polythene. Stress that they must **never** place bags over their heads or cover their mouths and noses with the polythene film.*

## Previous skills/knowledge needed

It would be helpful if the children had experienced a variety of sorting activities prior to this lesson. (See 'Sort out your colour table' on page 51 and 'Feeling surfaces' on pages 14 and 15 in *Curriculum Bank Science, Key Stage One*.)

## Preparation

Make a collection of plastic items. These could include plastic bottles, carrier bags, toys, polythene film, nylon textiles, shoes, pens, rulers, classroom learning aids, counters, and perhaps, a telephone. (The choice is almost limitless!) Prepare a wordlist containing the language to be introduced in the activity. Leave sufficient space to include the children's suggestions during the lesson. Make copies of photocopiable page 111, one for each child.

Prepare an interactive display area for the collection which has an adjacent board on which the children's work can be mounted. Also prepare a couple of small name labels for each child. A small piece of Blu-Tack should be stuck to the back of each name tag.

Immediately before the lesson select a few objects which you think the children in your class will readily identify as being plastic. Have the chosen items concealed in a bag near you as you introduce the lesson.

## Resources needed

A collection of plastic items, paper, writing and drawing materials, name tags, a drawstring bag large enough to hold several of the plastic items, a word list of the properties of plastic, photocopiable page 111.

## Language to be introduced

Soft, bendy, flexible, hard, solid, rigid, transparent. There will also be other language appropriate to your particular collection.

## What to do

Bring the children together for the introduction but gather them away from the collection of plastic items. Talk to the children about the things that surround them in the classroom and assess their knowledge of materials from their answers. Use questions such as: *What can you tell me about the texture of wood, metal, paper, fabric? Is wood rigid or is it flexible? What do I mean by flexible?* These questions will direct the children to think about the properties of specific materials in preparation for the main part of this activity. When appropriate, reach into the bag in which you have concealed your chosen items. Pass the objects around so that the children can feel the textures. Try to get them to notice other properties such as whether they are shiny or dull. Ask the children to identify the material which has been used to make the item. Given the varied properties of plastics, some children may not agree that all the items drawn from your bag are plastic. Note those who are confused at this point so that you can support them later in the lesson.

Now ask the children to go on a plastic hunt. Tell them that you want them to try to identify one item made from plastic in the classroom. Hand out the name tags and explain that when they have selected an item they should stick their name tag to it and then return to the seating area. This will enable you to observe which children complete the task quickly and monitor whether they did in fact select an item made from plastic. After about two minutes bring the children back to the seating area.

Check that every child has selected an item made from plastic. Draw the children together and briefly share their choice of items. Why did they choose the item that they did? What properties of plastic does their chosen item have? Do all the children agree that the item is indeed made from plastic? Why/why not? Emphasize the range of different uses to which plastic is put.

Gather the children around your display of plastic objects. Explain that you want to make a 'plastic world' display but you need some drawings and writing to accompany it. Hand out the second set of name tags to each child and tell them to select an object from the display and to stick their name tags on their chosen objects. Tell them that you would like them to produce some work about their chosen plastic item. Give each child a copy of photocopiable page 111 and ask them to draw a detailed picture of their chosen item. Read them the words on your wordlist and explain that they are to use this list to help them describe the properties of their plastic item and to say how and for what purpose their item is used. Display the enlarged copy of your wordlist where all the children can see and refer to it.

If you run this as a group activity, and leave the children's name tags in place, each successive group will have a reduced set of items from which to choose. If you start with the group which needs the most support this will effectively create a differentiation in the activity.

At the end of the lesson, day or week draw the groups together to look at the collection and display. Count the number of different describing words for plastic that you have collected on the wordlist. Discuss the variety of different uses for which the material is used. If the number is within the age and ability of the class, count the number of different ways plastic has been used. Explain to the children that plastic has many properties and many uses. They have found 'x' number of uses so far. Leave them with a challenge by saying something like 'I wonder how many more you can find?'

Over a period of time encourage the children to add to the collection so that they gain a sense of ownership, but take care that precious items (such as favourite toys) are not included in the investigation carried out in the extension activity.

### Suggestion(s) for extension
Ask the children to investigate a selection of plastic items from the display. They can sort for rough and smooth or rigid and flexible (a variety of construction toys often provide a good range of properties to achieve this).

A larger scale plastic hunt could be carried out around the school building. This should add plastics used in the building trades to your collection and could introduce the topic of plastic and litter pollution.

### Suggestion(s) for support
Children needing support will benefit from being introduced to a limited range of plastics in the first instance. You could limit the range effectively by using plastic toys. Subsequently, one different use for plastic could be introduced at a time.

Least able children may need to return to sorting objects from a mixed set containing rock, wood and metal.

### Assessment opportunities
Note those children who are particularly able to identify a full range of uses for plastics. It is very unusual for children to accept that fabrics can have a plastic content. Ask the children to describe the properties of plastic: *How did you know it was made of plastic?*

### Display ideas
Display the collection of plastic objects alongside collections of other materials. The children's pictures can be displayed with photographs, pictures cut from magazines and other publications and posters with labels describing the use to which plastic has been put. Make a large list of the different uses of plastic. Complete the display with the title 'Plastic has lots of uses' in large lettering.

### Other aspects of the Science PoS covered
Experimental and Investigative Science 2a, 2b, 2c. Section 0 4a, 4b.

### Reference to photocopiable sheet
Photocopiable page 111 provides a space for the children to draw their selected plastic item. It also requires them to focus their thinking on the properties of plastic and the way in which their object has been used.

# DON'T BURST MY BUBBLE!

*To learn that some materials have different uses and use this concept to develop the skills of investigation.*

**†† ** *Class activity followed by group recording.*

🕐 *45–60 minutes.*

⚠ *Safety: If you are making your own bubble mixture you need to consider the children's skin sensitivity and exercise due caution. Take care that water and soap spilled on the floor do not constitute a Health and Safety risk. Keep a cloth, newspaper or paper towels to hand for mopping up spills. Make sure that there is plenty of space in the bubble blowing area.*

## Previous skills/knowledge needed

In order to encourage the children to focus on the investigation within this activity it is important that they have all previously played with bubble mixtures and experienced bubble blowing.

## Key background information

Once you have chosen your bubble mixture keep to the one mixture and make it all the same strength so as to reduce the variables and improve the 'fairness' of the investigation.

The greater the selection of bubble blowers the more demanding the investigation becomes. You will need to use your professional judgement here. If in doubt just use two different bubble blowers for the first lesson and extend the activity through the week by adding different types of blowers. (This activity may be best carried out outdoors but if you are working with a small group it could be an indoor activity.) Even if the children have had experience of blowing bubbles, some will try to catch the bubbles initially so allow time for this before you begin the activity in earnest.

## Preparation

Buy or mix your own bubble mixture and pour the mixture into shallow trays for use in the lesson. Mild washing-up liquid, children's shampoo and liquid hand-washing soap mixed with water can all be used quite successfully. The mixture does not need to be very strong, it is probably best to start with a weak mixture. Surprisingly, bubble bath does not seem to be very effective. The children should wear plastic aprons when carrying out this activity.

Prepare a few loops of wire to act as bubble blowers – garden wire and pipe cleaners are suitable – you can also use twist ties if you join several together. Collect some pots (for example yoghurt or cottage cheese tubs) and cut off the base of each pot. Empty washing up liquid bottles and plastic drinks bottles are also good for this

activity – wash thoroughly and cut off the base.

Before the lesson put out two different types of bubble blower with the trays of bubble mixture ready for the children to use. Put out several of each sort, enough for everyone in the group. Depending on the age and ability of the children, either put out two different types of wire bubble blower or one wire bubble blower and a 'cottage cheese' style blower (a pot with a hole in the base). Reserve all the other bubble blowers. Have examples of all the types you will be using ready to hand when you talk to the children away from the bubble blowing area. Make copies of photocopiable page 112, one for each child.

## Resources needed

A collection of bubble blowers (see 'Preparation', some commercially produced bubble blowers are useful for comparison), trays containing a shallow layer of well mixed bubble blowing liquid (margarine and ice-cream tubs will do instead of trays), mopping up cloths and plenty of towels, aprons, photocopiable page 112, board or flip chart. For the support activity – a camera (optional).

## Language to be introduced

Compare, test, bubble blower, bubble mixture. There are also opportunities to introduce language about the appearance of the bubbles, including transparent, translucent, spherical, rainbow coloured, reflection. You may also wish to introduce the language of forces: blow, push, changing shape, falling, gravity.

## What to do

Tell the children that you have made some bubble mixture for them. Allow the children a little time to enjoy bubble blowing before introducing the investigation. When you feel it is appropriate, draw them together away from the bubble mixture, but tell them to bring their bubble blowers with them. If the children are very young, do the bubble blowing part of the activity before playtime so that there is a natural break between the two halves of the lesson.

Talk to the children about the different bubbles they made. *Who made a good bubble?* Discuss why they thought it was a good bubble. Was it its size, its shape, how long it lasted, whether or not it floated in the air? Use the children's ideas of 'good' to draw up a simple definition. Next, look at the bubble makers which made these good bubbles. Which bubble blower was the best? Blow a few bubbles yourself to confirm the children's opinions. It should stop any disagreements!

Now introduce another bubble maker, for example the washing-up liquid blower. Ask the children to predict whether they think this blower will make a good bubble or not. Help them to articulate their reasoning. At this point you could write a few sentences with them on the board and take a vote on who does and does not think it will make a good bubble blower. Go with the children to the bubble blowing area and allow them to test the bubble blower. Question them as they carry out the investigation, extending their language as you do so. *Why is it a good bubble blower? Does it allow you to direct the force of your blow better? Is the blowing area larger or smaller?* If it does not make a good bubble ask them whether they think this is because they are using too much force when they blow. *Is the bubble blower too big or too small?* At

this stage, you can begin to link cause and effect together. For example: *This does not make a good bubble because the blowing area is too small.*

Afterwards, ask the children to confirm whether or not their predictions have been supported by the evidence. Were their predictions correct? Ask the children to choose another bubble blower and repeat the investigation: predict whether this bubble blower will create good bubbles, carry out the activity and conclude with what has been found out.

When the children have finished testing as many blowers as you wish, hand out copies of photocopiable page 112. Explain that you want them to mark the bubble blowers in order from the best blower to the worst. The children should give each blower a mark out of ten. Much discussion will be generated if one photocopiable sheet is given to a group of children to complete as they will all have to agree on the scoring.

## Suggestion(s) for extension

Ask the most able pupils to suggest their own designs for bubble blowers and then allow them to incorporate their ideas into the investigation. The introduction of two different bubble mixtures would make the investigation suitable for the most able pupils. You could also ask the children to predict what shape bubble they would get from a square bubble blower.

## Suggestion(s) for support

Some children may find the activity too distracting to allow them time to reflect on the science. Try taking photographs of the activity so that they can think about what they have done in more settled surroundings. Repeat the activity but blow the bubbles yourself and compare only two bubble blowers.

## Assessment opportunities

Make a note of those children who are able to suggest criteria for 'good bubbles' and apply the criteria to the investigation. Be aware of pupils who may be devising their own tests – they will be carrying out a systematic process (one which may differ from the way in which you would carry out the investigation). Ask the children if they can be sure that the comparisons being made are 'fair' and note those who are able/unable to communicate their findings.

## Display ideas

Display the children's findings alongside the comments you have noted when assessing the children. Wonderful display opportunities can also be gained from work on bubbles. If this lesson is one of a series on the theme of bubbles you could display close observational drawings, reflections, bubble paintings and the spectrum colours.

## Other aspects of the Science PoS covered

Physical Processes 2b, 2d. Experimental and Investigative Science 1a, 1b, 1c, 2a, 2b, 2c, 3a, 3b, 3c, 3d. Section 0 1a, 1b, 5b.

## Reference to photocopiable sheet

Photocopiable page 112 is a recording sheet on which the children can give their bubble makers scores out of ten. This will provide evidence of the 'best' and the 'worst' bubble maker.

# TIE YOURSELF IN KNOTS

*Materials are chosen for specific purposes based on their properties.*

✝✝ *Group activity.*

🕐 *30 minutes.*

## Previous skills/knowledge needed

The children would benefit from having sorted a collection of shoes for a variety of attributes before this lesson so you may like to carry out the activity 'Shoes' on page 12. This will help the children to sustain the focus on laces which is needed for this lesson. It would be helpful if the children had some skills in tying and lacing, perhaps developed through play activities with 'lacing toys'.

## Preparation

Make a collection of shoes and trainers that have laces laced in different ways. You will need one shoe for each child or one per pair. Prepare some lacing boards by punching holes in some thick cardboard or corrugated plastic. See the illustration on page 60. (A large 2-hole punch can be used for this if you do not have any other appropriate tool.) Make copies of photocopiable page 113, one for each child. Make a photocopy of the outline and stick it to card before cutting out and making the holes for threading. (You may like to enlarge this photocopiable sheet if you think it will make it easier for the children to use.)

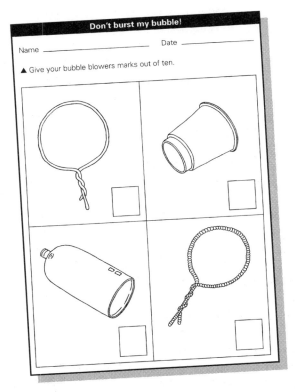

## Resources needed

A collection of differently laced shoes and trainers, laces (either new or used), lacing boards, a selection of materials – in addition to the real laces – for the children to investigate as lacing materials. These materials could include: string, thin garden wire, art straws, raffia, wool, and some materials which would be totally unsuitable for lacing, for example strips of wooden doweling or lengths from a plastic construction toy. A camera (optional), photocopiable page 113.

## Language to be introduced

Lace, knot, weave, bendy, flexible, rigid, tie, thread.

## What to do

Gather the children around your collection of shoes and ask them to choose one each. (Alternatively, you could allow them to work with a partner.) Tell them to look very carefully at the laces as you will be asking them to describe them to you. After you have listened to a few descriptions, focus some questions on what would make a good lace. *What does the lace need to do?* Draw out words or phrases such as 'thread', 'bend', 'flexible', 'not rigid or stiff' and 'weave'. At this point you may wish to get the children to compare two shoes, looking for similarities and differences between the laces and the eyelets through which they pass. There are many variations in laces and this can provide a stimulus for a great deal of useful discussion. If you do this, you may wish to stop here and then continue with the rest of this activity at another time.

Next, tell the children that you will be asking them to predict which materials would make good laces. Hold up your examples one at a time and ask the children to vote or sort them into sets. You may like to record this activity by creating a chart of the votes or photographing the completed sets. Finally, give the children some lacing boards or the card shoe templates made from photocopiable page 113 and ask them to try the materials to test their predictions.

Draw the lesson together by choosing some particularly good examples of children's work, reinforcing the ideas that laces need to be made of flexible materials.

## Suggestion(s) for extension

One attribute necessary for good laces is that they slide well through the eyelets. Ask more able children to show you which materials slide easily through the holes. They could then put the laces in rank order, for example 'Good lace', 'Not so good', 'Will not lace'. The children could go on to invent different ways of lacing.

## Suggestion(s) for support

An adult helper may be useful as long as the 'helpful' adult does not do all the lacing! Limit the number of eyelets in your lacing boards so that the less able children do not find the task too daunting.

## Assessment opportunities

While the children are sorting the lacing materials, make a note of those who are particularly able/unable to correctly predict which materials would make good laces. Note also those children who understand that the shape of some materials can be changed through bending.

## Display ideas
Display the lacing boards alongside the collection of shoes. The 'random-holed' boards look particularly good when completed in a variety of different coloured wools or raffia.

## Other aspects of the Science PoS covered
Physical Processes 2a, 2b. Section 0 4a.

## Reference to photocopiable sheet
Photocopiable page 113 provides an outline of a shoe which can be used as a template to make a board for the children to practise lacing and threading.

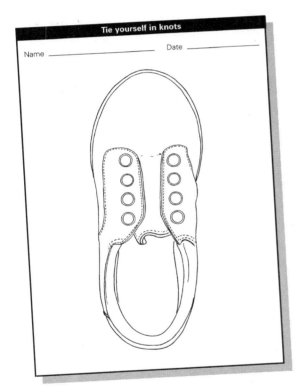

 **GLOVES TO KEEP YOU WARM**

*Materials are chosen for specific purposes because of their properties.*

†† *Class introduction followed by group investigation.*

🕐 *45 minutes.*

⚠ *Safety: Ice bags can be heavy. Make sure that the children are sitting during the investigation so that if the ice bag is dropped, it will not land from a great height on anyone's toes.*

## Previous skills/knowledge needed
It would be helpful if all the children had been outside with you on a cold day wearing just one glove each and had then talked about why the glove had kept their hand warm.

## Key background information
This lesson is best carried out during the winter months when the children can bring their own gloves to school.

## Preparation
Make a collection of materials which can be worn like a glove (see 'Resources needed'). Make a simple glove out of tissue paper and another from medium thickness card. Freeze some ice blocks (you can either use ones used for cool boxes or freeze water in plastic bags). Make copies of photocopiable page 114, one for each child. Make an enlarged copy for use with the class.

### Resources needed

Some good quality children's gloves that will fit your pupils' hands (or ask the children to bring in their own gloves). A collection of materials to be compared with the real glove. This collection could include: plastic bags, paper bags, bubble wrap, a variety of textiles (stapled to make a bag shape). A glove made from tissue paper and one made from medium thickness card. If possible, an assortment of protective gloves, for example gardening gloves, rubber gloves. Ice blocks. Photocopiable page 114.

### Language to be introduced

Temperature, bendy, flexible, rigid, soak up, absorb, keep warm, insulate.

### What to do

Talk to the children about gloves and why they are worn. Use some of your collection to demonstrate the different uses. Discuss why the materials have been used to make the gloves in your collection. Show the children the gloves made from rubber. Explain that these are the type of gloves a person would wear to do the washing-up. Ask the children why they think the gloves are made from rubber. Some children will be able to tell you that it is because rubber is waterproof so that when a person does the washing-up their hands will not get wet. Next, show the children the gardening gloves and discuss the reasons why these gloves are made from a different material. (They keep hands clean; they are flexible so that fingers can still be moved; they protect them from thorns, and so on).

Explain the investigation at this point. Tell the children that they are going to investigate which material would make a good glove. Ask what type of glove would keep their hands warm on a cold day. Ask a child to hold up his or her own glove or, alternatively, hold up a glove from your collection. Ask the children to predict whether the glove would be good for keeping hands warm. Do the children know what material the glove is made from? Next, hold up the rubber glove and the gloves you have made from paper and card. Do the children think that the gloves made from paper, card or rubber will keep their hands warm? Record their responses on your enlarged copy of photocopiable page 114, putting a tick or a cross in each box.

Now test the gloves by asking different children to compare the insulating properties of the two gloves by holding ice packs in their hands. On one hand they should wear a 'proper glove – one intended to keep their hands warm – and on the other hand either the paper, card or latex glove. Which hand feels the cold first? Show the children where to record the results on photocopiable page 114. Test another glove made from a different material in the same way. The children can then continue the investigation in groups. Photocopiable page 114 will guide the children to make predictions on whether the glove is made from a suitable material to keep hands warm before carrying out the investigation.

When all of the children have had the opportunity to complete the investigation, gather them together to discuss what they have discovered. Did they find gloves that were made from suitable material to keep their hands warm? Which materials were good for this purpose? Put these gloves together in a set. Were there some gloves that did not keep their hands warm very well? Which materials were used to make these gloves? Were these materials suitable for another purpose? Put these gloves into a set and label it according to the properties of the gloves, for example 'These gloves are made from a material that helps to keep our hands clean and dry.' Label the gloves that are good at keeping hands warm 'These gloves have been made from the material chosen because it keeps our hands warm.'

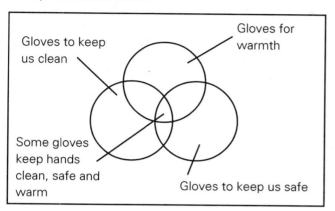

Talk to the children about the materials used to make the gloves in each set and record which materials are suitable for keeping hands warm. Explain to the children again at this point that materials are chosen for specific purposes, and that these materials were chosen because they are good for keeping hands warm and fitted that purpose.

### Suggestion(s) for extension
In addition to testing for insulation properties the children could also test the materials for other criteria such as keeping hands dry and warm; keeping hands warm but flexible. This would mean the children would also have to test all the materials for insulation and/or absorbency or insulation and/or flexibility. The children should repeat the test but record different evidence. Would card make good gloves? (No, the card is not flexible.) Would tissue paper make good gloves? (No, tissue paper would disintegrate when it became wet.) Tell the children to observe and record what happens when the gloves are tested out.

### Suggestion(s) for support
Several aspects of this lesson are open-ended and would consequently challenge many children. Try reducing the range of materials investigated. You could call the investigation 'Why don't we wear paper bags to keep our hands warm?' This is a very effective activity on a snowy day when the children can make snowballs.

### Assessment opportunities
There are two areas for assessment in this lesson:
▲ the children's understanding of the materials;
▲ their ability to draw conclusions from what happened and to say what they found out.
Both will be revealed as the children carry out the investigation. Watch for those children who are able to isolate one necessary characteristic for gloves such as

flexibility, insulation, absorbency. Make a note of the children who use the recorded evidence to say whether it supports their predictions. Which children are able to use the evidence to form a conclusion and say what they found out? Most children will require some assistance through your questioning as they develop their investigations.

### Display ideas
Display the collection of gloves and label them with questions such as 'Which gloves might be used by a builder?'

Mount pieces of the materials which have been investigated by the children and write the children's comments alongside. 'Jamie thinks this will make a good glove because...'

### Other aspects of the Science PoS covered
Experimental and Investigative 1a, 1b, 1c, 2a, 2b, 2c, 3a, 3c, 3d. Science Section 0 1a, 1b, 2a, 3a, 4a, 4b, 5b.

### Reference to photocopiable sheet
Photocopiable page 114 is a recording sheet which requires the children to predict and test whether a glove is made from a material suitable for keeping hands warm. The sheet can be used to discuss whether the evidence supports their predictions, and can be used as a check sheet for sorting the gloves into sets of good and not good hand warmers!

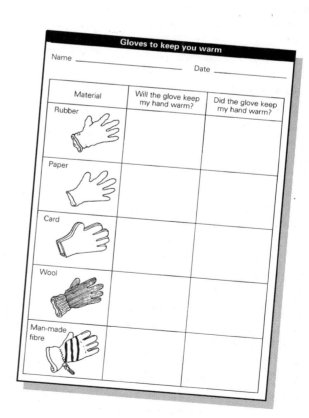

# BEND YOUR IMAGE

*Materials are chosen for specific purposes. Some materials and their purpose can be changed by bending.*

†† *Class or group activity.*

🕐 *30 minutes.*

⚠ *Safety: Do not allow the children to handle glass mirrors. This activity can cause excitement and mirrors can easily be broken. There is a range of good quality plastic mirrors available for purchase in most educational catalogues.*

## Previous skills/knowledge needed

Children should have had the opportunity to look at themselves in a mirror and to discuss their reflection using the appropriate language.

## Key background information

It may be appropriate to explain to the children that when a mirror is bent, the light is reflected in a different direction. This bends the image.

## Preparation

Make a collection of bendy mirrors. Try making a large reflective surface by coating a piece of thick card, hardboard or corrugated plastic board with an even layer of good quality foil. It may take a little time and effort sourcing the best foil but the results can be very impressive. (Some foils are textured and thus do not make the best reflective surface.) Reflective material used to cover car windows is effective but expensive and can be bought at most good motor accessory shops. Educational suppliers stock different-coloured foils. This can extend the activities to fit with those suggested in 'Sort out your colour table' on page 51. Make copies of photocopiable page 115, one for each child.

## Resources needed

One large-plane mirror, a collection of bendy mirrors, a large flexible mirror which will bend in a variety of ways, a sufficient number of small-plane mirrors and concave/convex mirrors for each member of the group. You should include at least one glass mirror for use by yourself. Photocopiable page 115.

## Language to be introduced

Reflect, reflection, distorted, image, mirror, concave, convex, bend, long, thin, fat, wide.

## What to do

Show the children a large-plane, plastic mirror and talk to them about what they can see in it. Is what they see affected by where they are sitting? Can they see their own image, another person or the reflection of an object in another part of the room? Move the mirror to a different position. What can the children see now? Discuss the reasons why they can see a different image. Explain that

this is because the mirror has changed position, therefore the image has changed.

Now ask the children what they think would happen to the image if the mirror was bent. Use the large flexible mirror so that you can bend it in a number of ways. Bend the mirror backwards to make a convex mirror. Explain to the children that you have created a convex mirror, a mirror which bends outwards. Let the children take turns to look at their distorted reflection in the mirror. Ask them what they can see. What has happened to the image? Is it a clear reflection or is the image distorted? Is the image fat, thin, short, and so on? Explain that the image is being reflected differently because the mirror has been bent. Next, bend the mirror into a concave shape. Explain to the children what you have made and that a concave mirror is one which bends inwards – like a cave. Ask the children to describe their reflection now. Do they notice that some or all of their image is upside down? Some children may be able to suggest why this is or be ready for an explanation. Hand out the bendy mirrors and allow the children the opportunity to try the activity for themselves.

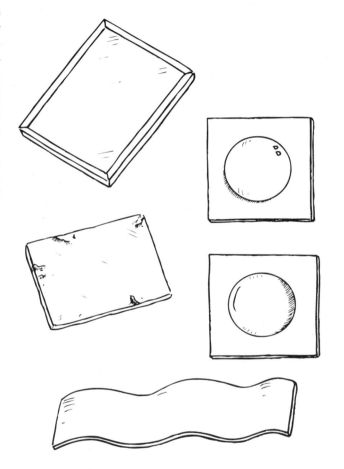

After a few minutes draw the group together and show them the glass mirror. Ask them if they know what their mirrors at home are made from. Can they guess what your mirror is made from? If the children do not give the correct answer, you may like to tell them so that you can discuss whether or not it is possible to bend a glass mirror.

Now give the children the concave/convex mirrors. Ask them to predict what the images will be like in both the concave and the convex sides. To draw the lesson together, reinforce the teaching points by recapping the following:

▲ the different materials used for mirrors (such as foil, glass and plastic);

▲ the materials we can bend (recap with the children that they have looked at bendy plastic mirrors and glass mirrors which do not bend. The plastic concave/convex mirrors you looked at may also have been bendy.);

▲ what happens to the image when the material is (or has been) bent.

Give each child a copy of photocopiable page 115 and look at it with them. Explain that you want them to draw the reflections they can see in the concave and convex mirrors It is best to do this part of the activity in small groups as there may be some children with less well-developed literacy skills who need help.

### Suggestion(s) for extension
Extend the intellectual challenge of this lesson by introducing shiny, reflective spoons. This adds an extra material in the form of metal. It also adds an object which is difficult to bend (but which has already been 'bent' for us).

Show the children a spoon. Assess who knows that the spoon is made from metal. Ask the children to predict what their reflection will be like in both sides of the spoon. Now allow the children time to try this out for themselves.

### Suggestion(s) for support
Some children may have had little experience of mirrors. Use the collection of mirrors as an interactive display allowing them free play with the materials for a few days before the lesson.

### Assessment opportunities
Note those children who are able to identify which materials can be bent to alter the image. Listen carefully as children describe what they can see in their mirrors. Are they describing in detail? Have they tried holding the mirror close to their faces or holding it from different angles? Ask the children to find objects that will reflect an image upside down. Make a note of those children who automatically look for an object with a concave reflective surface.

### Display ideas
Compile the children's work on mirrors into a class book. You can also incorporate mirrors into the book. The children love to read and reread these books. A torch can also be left with the display in order to stimulate and encourage further investigation.

## Other aspects of the Science PoS covered

Physical Processes 2a, 2b. Experimental and Investigative Science 2a, 2b, 2c, 3a, 3b, 3c. Section 0 1b, 4a.

## Reference to photocopiable sheet

Photocopiable page 115 is a simple recording sheet which the children can use to draw the reflections they see in a convex and a concave mirror. The simple cloze procedure will support the children's understanding.

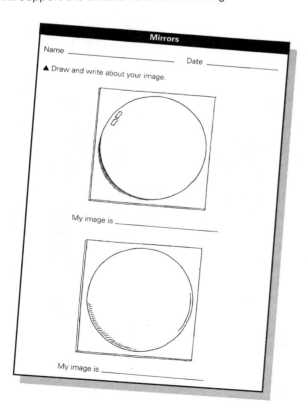

## SPRINGY THINGS

*Some materials and their characteristics can be changed by bending.*

†† *Group activity.*

🕐 *30 minutes.*

## Previous skills/knowledge needed

It would be helpful if the children had experienced playing with springy materials through the exploration of toys and games, for example 'Flip Frog'. (This is a game produced by MERIT. It is an enhanced form of tiddlywinks in which frogs are flipped into their pond.) They should also have had the opportunity to see and handle springs. These are available in packs from science and technology suppliers.

## Preparation

Collect all the materials needed for the lesson in trays so that they are easily accessible to you but not available to the children for 'indiscriminate' free play.

Cut some card into strips about 2cm wide and 6 cm long. These will be folded in a concertina pattern to form springs. Also cut some lengths of wire long enough to be coiled around a pencil.

## Resources needed

A collection of springs. It would be helpful if some of these springs could be kept in their places of use, for instance inside a torch or a ballpoint pen, so that you can show how springs are used. Card of varying thickness (six sheet and three sheet are suitable thicknesses). Wire which can easily be coiled by your pupils. Thin electrical wire of the sort to be found with your school's science electrical resources is often suitable. Otherwise obtain some 'springy' garden wire from a DIY shop. Pencils to coil the wire around. You may need some tape to help children start the coils off (stick one end of the wire to the pencil to hold it still).

## Language to be introduced
Bend, fold, coil, spring, bounce, squash, springs back into shape.

## What to do
Talk to the children about the springs in your collection. (The springs you will be focusing on will be 'compression springs' – that is springs that work by pushing and releasing so that they spring back into shape. Do not allow the children to stretch the springs as this can distort them and ruin them.) Draw out descriptions from the children as to where they might find springs in everyday life. Show them the ball point pen and/or the torch (or any item you have managed to obtain that has a spring in it you can show to the children) and get them to describe the functions of the springs. Disassemble the objects if possible and put them back together again.

Give each child a small strip of thin card and show them how to make a simple spring by folding the card in a concertina fashion. Allow the children time to play with their springs. For some children this may be sufficient for one lesson or you may decide to allow them to play a game at this point similar to tiddly-winks. Allow the children to compress their card springs, release them and watch as they jump across the table. A simple race can be played

to see who can 'jump' their card across the table first, or who can get their card to jump the furthest or highest.

If the children are able to sustain interest, call them together and show them how to coil the wire around the pencil to form a spring. (Extra adult help may be needed to assist with the folding of the card and coiling of wire. You could possibly prepare these in advance but it would be much better for the children to be involved in the making of their own springs.) Relate this spring to the ones seen in the torch and/or pen. Explain that the torch or pen works in a similar way to the card spring. To make it work, the spring is compressed and when it is released, it springs back into shape.

To draw the lesson to a close, emphasize the main learning objective by comparing the materials. Show the children the card in its unfolded state and compare how it looks when it is folded. The bending has altered the shape of the card. In so doing, the characteristics of the material have been changed.

## Suggestion(s) for extension
Make a collection of materials that spring back into shape after being squashed or bent; items could include a bath sponge, a sponge-filled cushion, coiled wire such as that found on a telephone receiver or headphones, guitar string, a rubber ball. Include items that use springs to make them work such as clothes pegs, door handles, locks and clocks. Allow the children to disassemble these if possible. Encourage the children to add to the collection and use it to reinforce and extend their concept and experience of materials.

## POPCORN

*Many materials change when heated.*

†† *Class or group activity.*

🕐 *30 minutes.*

⚠ *Safety: Follow school safety guidelines on the use of microwaves or cookers in the classroom.*

### Previous skills/knowledge needed

Any experience of cooking and food preparation would be helpful.

### Key background information

It is best to do this activity using a microwave and microwaveable popping corn with small groups of children who can all see what is happening when heat is applied. The corn can be 'popped' in the bag or in a see-through pyrex basin.

### Preparation

Arrange access to cooking facilities and organize additional adult help.

### Resources needed

Popcorn (you will need two bags, the sort in a sealed bag is best), salt, frozen sweetcorn or a tin of sweetcorn, a corn on the cob, cooking utensils (a little butter if cooking on a stove), cooker or microwave, paper, writing and drawing materials.

### Language to be introduced

Corn, pop, expand, cook, heat, hard, soft, squashy, yellow, white.

### What to do

Begin the lesson by looking at the corn on the cob. Assess the children's level of understanding. Do they know that the corn has been grown on a plant? Do they recognize it as being the sweetcorn which they may eat at home? Show them some frozen corn or tinned corn as a comparison. Now look at the corn which you are going to pop. Explain to the children that they are going to make popcorn and that they are going to do this by heating corn.

Open one of the bags of corn and pass the contents around for the children to touch. Ask them to describe its texture. If they do not mention it, draw the children's attention to the hardness of the corn. You may also like to compare it to the corn from the cob. Ask them to try to squeeze the corn. Can it be squashed? Explain that the reason they cannot squash it is because the water has been taken out; the corn has been dried. What can they tell you about its colour? Again, explain that it is a darker yellow than the corn on the cob because this corn is dried. When you are happy that the children understand this, ask them to predict what will happen when the corn is

### Suggestion(s) for support

If some children are finding it difficult to grasp the concept of springiness then try taking them outside where they can be 'springy' themselves and bunny hop or frog-leap around the playground. Discuss with them the way they change the shape of their body and compare this to the springs.

### Assessment opportunities

Record the names of those children who understand how a compression spring works. In particular, note those children who are able to identify items found in everyday life that use springs, such as pegs, torches, ballpoint pens and staplers.

### Display ideas

Add cut out card names, shapes or characters to the springs and mount them horizontally or vertically to form a display board or table.

### Other aspects of the Science PoS covered

Physical Processes 2a 2b 2c 2d. Section 0 1a, 2a, 4a.

heated. Some children may know through previous experience what may happen. In any case, you can record the children's predictions as a table of results or as a simple bar chart.

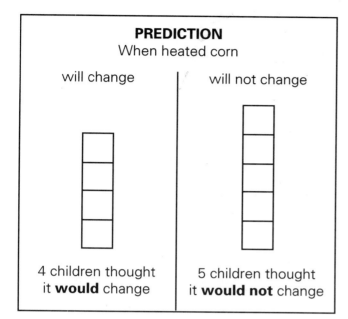

**PREDICTION**
When heated corn

| will change | will not change |
|---|---|
| 4 children thought it **would** change | 5 children thought it **would not** change |

Now it is time to cook the popcorn. Organize the children into groups so that each group can stand in front of the microwave and see the changes that take place. They will also be able to hear the changes, either as the bag expands or as the corn pops! If necessary, after the corn has been microwaved, remove the popped corn from the bag and empty it into a bowl. When the popcorn is cool enough to be handled, allow the children to eat some. Ask them to tell you how the corn has changed. What can they tell you about the colour? Is the corn still the same shape? Is the corn hard or soft? Ask the children to squeeze the corn now. What are their responses? Is the corn easy to squash now? Does the corn take up more room? Explain that the corn has expanded and that it has changed because it has been heated. Can the children think of other foods or materials which change when they are heated?

Hand out some paper and writing and drawing materials and tell the children to record their responses by drawing before and after pictures. These can be before and after pictures of the popcorn, or pictures of any foods that change when heated.

### Suggestion(s) for extension
More able children may be able to use secondary sources to research other materials which change when heated such as clay, and others which you cannot handle or demonstrate such as molten metals, rocks in volcanoes and materials which burn. Very able children could look at reversible and irreversible changes.

### Suggestion(s) for support
Try melting chocolate (see the activity 'Melting chocolate'

on page 65 of *Curriculum Bank Science, Key Stage One*) and cooking sponge mixtures to provide children with a greater range of experience. This should help to develop their understanding of the concept that many materials change when heated.

### Assessment opportunities
This lesson allows you the opportunity to assess children's understanding of their world as well as the effect on some materials of heat. Note those children who can/cannot trace the origins of the corn back to its plant source. Which children understand that we derive much of our food from plants? Similarly, at the end of the lesson, note those who are able to use their general knowledge and wider conceptual development to explain the connections between what has gone on in this lesson with other changes caused by heating.

### Display ideas
The children can create before and after pictures. You can either use real corn and popcorn or, if you prefer not to use food, coloured dough can be used to represent unpopped corn and wood chippings to represent popcorn.

### Other aspects of the Science PoS covered
Experimental and Investigative Science 2a, 2b, 2c, 3a, 3c. Section 0 1a,1c, 2a, 5a. Life Processes and Living Things 3c.

# BURNT TOAST AND HARD CHEESE

**Materials change when heated.**

♦♦ *Class activity.*

⊕ *40 minutes.*

⚠ *Safety: The children should follow the school's policy on food preparation and hygiene. Hands should be washed and clothes covered with suitable aprons. Make sure the children are aware of the dangers of cooking using direct heat. Keep a fire blanket close at hand in case of fire. Do not let the children handle the melted cheese until it has cooled. Check whether any children suffer from any food allergies before the lesson.*

## Previous skills/knowledge needed

Experience of cookery and food preparation would be helpful. The contents of this lesson supports the activity 'Popcorn' on page 68.

## Preparation

Arrange access to cooking facilities and organize additional adult support. This lesson includes references to burning. It is important to make sure that you know whether any of the children in your class have suffered burns so that you are able to talk sensitively about these issues. Make copies of photocopiable page 116, one for each child. Make copies of photocopiable page 117 for those children carrying out the support activity.

## Resources needed

A loaf of frozen sliced white bread. A freezer, fridge or coolbox to keep the bread in a frozen state. Grated or thinly sliced Cheddar cheese, cutlery and plates, a grill, cling film or plastic food bags, several large sheets of paper and a felt-tipped pen, photocopiable page 116. For the support activity – photocopiable page 117 (optional), scissors, blank paper.

## Language to be introduced

Grill, grilled, grilling, frozen, hard, soft, defrosted, solid, melted, toasting, toasted, browning, browned, burnt.

## What to do

Explain to the children that they are going to learn about the way in which things change when they are heated. Draw on their own knowledge of melting. Ask them what will happen if ice-cream is not put into a freezer, or if you hold a smartie in your hand for a long time. Can the children tell you about other things which will melt when heated? Most, if not all, will have experience of ice-creams, iced lollies, butter and so on. Write their suggestions on a large piece of paper for later use in a display.

Next, draw on their knowledge of burning. Ask: *Which materials burn when you heat them?* Again, most children will know about paper, toast and other foodstuffs. Write these words on another sheet of paper to form a complementary list. Ask those children taking part in the food preparation to wash their hands and put on their cooking aprons. Take the frozen loaf out of the coolbox and show the children that it is frozen. Pass the loaf around the children so that they can feel how solid the frozen bread is.

Talk to the children about what happens when you heat a loaf of bread which has been frozen. Focus on the change of state: the change from being frozen to being defrosted. Take a few slices of bread from the end of the loaf and pass them around the children who have clean hands. Ask them to hold the slice between their hands. Do they notice that the state of the bread is changing because of the heat of their hands? Brainstorm with the children words that describe the changes taking place. Make a before and after list of the children's suggestions. For example, on the 'before' list you can write 'The bread is hard, solid, cold'. On the 'after' list you could write 'The bread is soft, squashy, warm'. Explain to the children that the bread is defrosting and that the heat is changing its state.

Leave a few slices of bread on a plate to defrost. You may wish to note the time with the children so that you can see how long they take to defrost. Cover the bread with a plate and emphasize the need for hygiene.

Put the grill on to heat up. In the meantime, talk to the children about cooking and safety. Toast some of the bread on one side only. Encourage the children to tell you when they think the toast will be cooked. Make sure they understand that in this instance the heating process is not 'melting'. This process is called 'browning', 'toasting', 'grilling', or more generally 'cooking'. Toast a sufficient number of slices so that each child has a slice, then ask them to compare the toasted side with the untoasted side. What do they think the brown colour is? Why are some areas of the bread browner than others? What would happen if the toast was left under the grill for too long? Again, you may like to make a before and after list of the children's suggestions to record the changes in state.

Now go on to add the cheese to the untoasted side. Ask the children to predict what will happen when the cheese is grilled. Do they think it will take longer to grill the cheese than it did to toast the bread? Reinforce the concept that this cooking process relies on the fact that the cheese will melt when heated. Can the children think of other meals which contain melted cheese?

Refer back to the list you made of the children's suggestions as to which foods melt. If appropriate, when the cheese has cooled, allow the children to eat the cheese on toast, then conclude the activity by returning to your sheets of vocabulary which you produced during the lesson. One sheet should contain words about melting, and the other words about burning. Add the words 'cheese' and 'bread' if they are not already included. Spend a short time recalling the materials which melt when heated and the materials which burn when heated.

Emphasize the learning objective that all these materials changed when they were heated.

Hand out copies of photocopiable page 116 and go through it with the children. In the first picture they should colour in the slice of bread to show how it looked when it was untoasted. In the second picture they should colour in the bread to show the changes that took place after it was browned.

### Suggestion(s) for extension

Try boiling water in a Pyrex cup or bowl in the microwave. This adds a third effect of heating. You could use the water to make a cup of coffee for a visiting parent helper or, if it is allowed to cool a little, to dissolve a jelly. The more able children should then be able to explain that heating can cause materials to change by melting and burning, and can aid dissolving.

### Suggestion(s) for support

Use photocopiable page 116 as a support sheet to reinforce the learning objective. Give the children an uncooked slice of bread, talk about its properties and as the children make their suggestions, record them together on the first picture of the slice of bread either by colouring or labelling. Next, grill the bread on one side. When it has browned, place it on a plate in the centre of the group so that all the children can see it. Again, talk about the changes that have taken place as a result of heating the bread. Reinforce the fact that the bread was heated. Record the changes together that have taken place on the second picture. If you wish, melt some cheese on the uncooked side for the children to enjoy, but do not introduce the concept of melting at this point. This aspect of the lesson can be carried out at another time.

Alternatively, you may like to give the children copies of photocopiable page 117. These show pictures of bread in various stages, from frozen bread through to cheese on toast. The children have to cut out the pictures and paste them on to a sheet of paper in the correct order.

### Assessment opportunities
Check to see which children can use the language of heating correctly. The English language is very rich in this area and your questioning can often reveal limited knowledge of the vocabulary. Make an assessment about each child based both on their use of language and also on their overall conceptual development. The use of photocopiable page 116 should help.

### Display ideas
Show the process of heating from defrosting the loaf through browning under the grill to melting the cheese. The children can make large cut-out pictures for the display, using an enlargement of photocopiable page 116 labelled appropriately. In addition, you can display the words which you have recorded for melting and burning.

### Other aspects of the Science PoS covered
Experimental and Investigative Science 2a, 2b, 2c, 3a, 3b, 3c, 3d, 3f. Section 0 1a, 1b, 2a, 2b, 3a, 4a, 4b, 5a, 5b.

### Reference to photocopiable sheets
Photocopiable page 116 allows the children to record before and after pictures of their slice of bread, while photocopiable page 117 is a cut and paste activity. The children should cut out the pictures before pasting them in the correct order to show the sequence of change from frozen bread through to toasted cheese.

# Physical processes

This section of the book provides lesson plans that will help teachers deliver the Physical Processes aspect of Science. Lessons are included to cover Electricity, Forces, Motion, Light and Sound. Within each lesson plan considerable emphasis has been placed on the development of the children's observational skills. We have also been careful to relate the activities to young children's knowledge of physical phenomena.

All the teaching activities in this section of the book make use of common, everyday physical processes. The materials needed can be easily collected. If you wish, the children can be involved in the generation of some collections of materials. This can add to their sense of excitement and involvement.

As with all practical scientific investigation, the study of physical processes carries some element of risk. We would urge teachers to carry out risk assessments as part of their planning to ensure that the activities are safe for their own school's particular circumstances. Health and Safety can also be included in each lesson as the children are helped to learn how to control risks for themselves.

## BATTERIES MUST BE INCLUDED!

*An electrical device will not work if there is a break in the circuit.*
†† *Group activity.*
🕐 *30 minutes.*
⚠ *Safety: Rechargeable batteries should be avoided as they get extremely hot if short circuited. Double pin, 4.5 volt batteries are suitable for use with young children (Ever Ready Type 1289).*

### Previous skills/knowledge needed

Children should have carried out work on identifying everyday appliances that use electricity, and the associated safety issues should have been dealt with. The activities entitled 'Electricity and safety' and 'Using electricity' on pages 68 and 69 of *Curriculum Bank Science, Key Stage One* contain lessons on these subjects. Children should also have made their own simple circuits using wire, batteries and bulbs. See *Curriculum Bank Science, Key Stage One*, pages 71–73 for suitable activities.

### Preparation

Make a collection of torches which are sufficiently sturdy to stand being dismantled and put back together. One torch per child is ideal but the lesson will work with one between two children. As the torches will be dismantled, and to keep the individual components safe, it is a good idea to put each torch in a separate drawer tray for this activity. Gather together the equipment needed to make a circuit. Make sure that it all works when it is assembled.

### Resources needed

A collection of torches, blank paper/photocopiable page 118, writing and drawing materials, a battery, a small amount of kitchen foil, three crocodile leads and a bulb in a bulb holder. If you are using a 4.5 v battery it is suggested you use 3.5 v bulbs. For the extension activity – a selection of wires, bulbs, buzzers, switches and batteries.

### Language to be introduced

Bulb, battery, switch, wire, circuit, switch on, switch off, broken circuit, connection, complete circuit.

### What to do

Recap with the children the previous work that has been carried out on what electricity is used for, making bulbs light and safety. Next, show the children the wires, battery and bulb, and ask one of them to tell you how they could be used to make the bulb light. Assemble the circuit and check that different children can 'switch off' the light by breaking the circuit in different places. Set them the challenge of finding a way of switching off the light without touching the wires, for example by disconnecting the battery or unscrewing the bulb. Explain that the circuit has been broken, therefore the light does not work. Ask the children to explain what is happening when the circuit is broken. Encourage them to use the correct language as they explain, for example; 'I have switched off the light by breaking the circuit.' 'The circuit is broken because the wires are not touching.' 'The electricity cannot flow because the circuit is broken.'

Now introduce the concept of a simple switch. Place a small piece of kitchen foil between two wires in the circuit. (See the illustration below). Demonstrate to the children how the circuit can be broken by breaking the piece of foil in two. You can then use the foil as a simple switch, pressing the pieces together to make the bulb light and allowing them to spring apart to switch off the light.

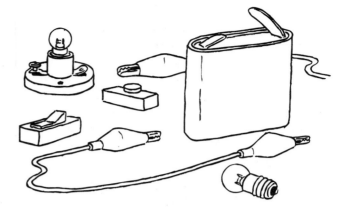

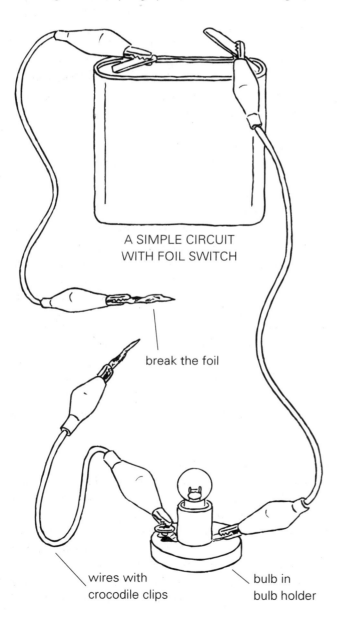

A SIMPLE CIRCUIT
WITH FOIL SWITCH

break the foil

wires with
crocodile clips

bulb in
bulb holder

Now take a torch and examine it with the children. Ask the children if they can explain in what way the torch is the same as the circuit with the bulb. (The switch makes the circuit whole, or completes the circuit, and the bulb lights.) Hand out the torches and allow pupils some time to dismantle and reassemble them. If you have sufficient torches allow the children to have one each but take care that the individual components are kept with the torch to which they belong. To draw the lesson together, check to see how many different ways the children can find to switch off the torch. If you have different torches in your collection there may well be different ways of switching them off. Can the children see how the torches all contain similar parts? Can each child explain what is happening when the torches are switched on and off? Can they explain that when the torch is switched off the circuit has been broken and therefore the torch does not work?

Ask the children to draw a picture of the inside of their torch showing how the circuit needs to be complete for the torch to light. Alternatively, hand out copies of photocopiable page 118 for the children to complete.

### Suggestion(s) for extension
Give the children a selection of wires, bulbs, buzzers, a switch and a battery and ask them to construct a model containing these components. You may like to tell them that it is a light to light up a dark place (see 'Playing in the dark' on page 89). When the children have all completed their models, ask them to tell the rest of the group about how their models work and to show what happens when the circuit is broken. Do their models still work?

### Suggestion(s) for support
Give the children opportunities to make circuits containing buzzers, motors and bulbs. A classroom assistant would be useful to help them articulate what happens every time the circuit is broken.

### Assessment opportunities
Make a note of those children who are able to construct a circuit and can explain that a complete circuit is needed to make their model work. Do they understand that if the

circuit is broken then the model will not work. Other children may be able to describe how the circuit inside a toy/game/torch makes the buzzer sound/bulb work.

## Opportunities for IT

Carry out a survey of electrical items in each classroom. Record the data on a simple data handling program, recording the information onto a block graph or simple spreadsheet. You could also make a concept keyboard overlay which the children can use to place the electrical appliances found into the appropriate rooms. Which room has the most appliances and why?

## Display ideas

The children can draw or cut out pictures from magazines and make a collection of models which need a complete circuit to work. These can be displayed around a back cloth made up of a giant circuit within a torch or any other toy you have used to support the activity.

## Other aspects of the Science PoS covered

Section 0 2a, 2b, 3a, 5b. Experimental and Investigative Science 3a, 3d.

## Reference to photocopiable sheet

Photocopiable page 118 requires the children to write down whether the bulb in each circuit will work and to draw a circle around the break in the circuit. Their completed sheets will indicate whether they have understood the learning objective.

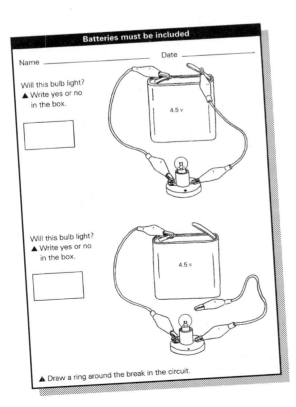

# PUSH AND PULL

*To identify pushes and pulls and understand that pushes and pulls are forces which make things start and stop.*

†† *Class or group activity.*

⏱ *45 minutes.*

⚠ *Safety: Always use an extra classroom helper when children are doing the activity outside the immediate classroom area. This adult can also be useful to reinforce the learning objective and to keep the children focused.*

## Preparation

Make a list of all the items inside the classroom that move by pushing, pulling and both for the additional helper to refer to during the activity. Prepare a large number of Post-it notes with 'Push', 'Pull' and 'Push and pull' written on them. Make copies of photocopiable page 119. Make copies of photocopiable page 120 for those children carrying out the support activity, or one enlarged copy.

## Resources needed

A large number of Post-it notes appropriately labelled, a push along toy car and a pull along toy, photocopiable page 119. For the support activity – photocopiable page 120.

## Language to be introduced

Move, start, stop, push, pull, change direction, force.

## What to do

Gather the children together into a circle. Show the children the toy car and explain that they are going to play a game called 'Catch it'. Choose a child who is sitting opposite you on the carpet and, saying that child's name, roll the car across the circle to her or him and invite the child to 'Catch it'. Ask that child to pick another child sitting opposite, roll the car and invite that child to 'Catch it'. All the children in the circle can say together, '1,2,3, Push'.

Continue with the game until all the children have had a turn to push and catch the car. Stress the fact that the children made the car move by pushing it. Place the car in front of you and explain that unless the car is pushed it will not start to move; it will stay still. Now introduce the pull along toy and place it in front of you. Does the toy start to move on its own? Why not? Invite the children to say whether the toy will need to be pushed or pulled to make it move. It may be appropriate to explain at this point that pushes and pulls are forces which make things start to move. Ask a child to demonstrate that when the toy is pulled it starts to move.

Challenge the children to find things in the classroom that need either a push or a pull to make them begin to move. Show the children the Post-it notes you have prepared and tell the children that they are to look

thoroughly around the classroom to find objects that need a push to move, objects that need a pull to move, and objects that can be moved by pushing and pulling. When they find an example of each item they must stick a label on it. It may be appropriate to find three examples as a class activity before the children go off in small groups to investigate.

Bring the children back together after a suitable period and talk about some of the objects they have labelled. Invite each child to name one object and explain whether it needs a push, a pull or both in order for it to move. Photocopiable page 119 can be used to record the things the children find. (You may like to complete one enlarged sheet with the whole class. Alternatively the children could complete one individually or one per group.) Count the number of objects labelled so far. Are the children surprised by the number? Did they think there would be more or fewer? Challenge them to find some more items to add to the list.

### Suggestion(s) for extension
More able children may challenge the 'push and pull' concept underlying this lesson and suggest that some things do not need pushes and pulls to make them start moving. For instance, they may suggest that a car on a slope does not need a push or a pull to start rolling. Challenge these children by helping them understand that the car does need to be pulled in order to be placed on the slope ready to roll. In the case of a toy car on a slope the 'pull' is provided when the person who placed it on the

slope lifts the car into the air. If the car has been lifted, force has been applied to overcome gravity. Alternatively, the car may be pulled (or dragged) up the slope. Challenge the children to put the car on the slope without pulling!

### Suggestion(s) for support
Some children will benefit from a more kinaesthetic approach to help them develop the concepts contained within this lesson. Use ride-on toys, footballs, large apparatus and hoops to develop the language of pushes and pulls. If you have access to nursery play equipment you may find a rocking horse or baby's cradle provide interesting opportunities for practical work. Talk about and complete photocopiable page 120 together.

### Assessment opportunities
The children's labelling exercise is an assessment activity in itself. Make a record of the children who can accurately identify a range of objects using the Post-it notes. As an additional check you could keep one item in reserve and ask individual children how they would label it. A good assessment object might be a pencil eraser. Ask the children to rub out a mark. Did they push, pull or do both?

### Opportunities for IT
The children can use a data handling package such as *Graphplot* or *Graphit* to record onto a block graph the number of objects found which require a push, pull or both forces to make them move. Which force moves the greatest number of objects?

## Display ideas

Put a set of objects on a display table and encourage the children to sort the collection into 'pushes', 'pulls' and 'pushes and pulls'. This could be set out in large sorting rings to create a Venn diagram. Display two large rings on a board behind so that they overlap and inside this stick the children's drawings and paintings of the objects they found. Reinforce the learning objective by completing the display together, asking the children into which section they would put each picture and why.

## Other aspects of the Science PoS covered

Physical Processes 2a, 2b. Experimental and Investigative Science 1a, 2b, 2c, 3a, 3b, 3c. Section 0 1a, 1b, 1d, 2a, 3a, 4a, 4b, 5b.

## Reference to photocopiable sheets

Photocopiable page 119 is a recording sheet onto which the children can record the objects they found either by writing the names or drawing pictures of the objects. Photocopiable page 120 contains pictures of a number of objects likely to be found in a classroom. The children are invited to label each picture with the correct force or forces needed to make the depicted object move.

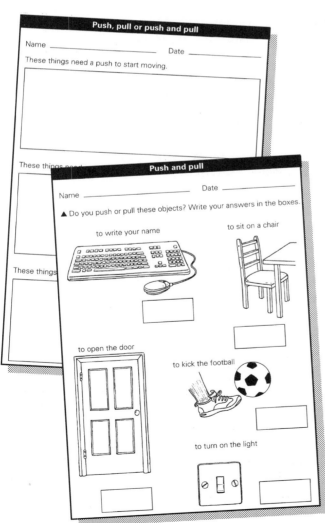

# ROCK, SWIVEL, SPIN AND SWING

*To describe the movement of familiar things.*

†† *Small groups.*

🕐 *30 minutes.*

⚠ *Safety: The use of a typist's chair in this lesson is only recommended if close one-to-one supervision is available. Take care that the swinging pendulums are not placed at the eye-level of the children who are taking part in the activity. You may judge it necessary to remove these items from your room immediately on completion of the lesson to prevent the possibility of unsupervised play.*

## Previous skills/knowledge needed

It would be useful if the children had carried out previous work on pushes and pulls. For suitable activities see the activities 'Pushes and pulls' on page 75 of *Curriculum Bank Science, Key Stage One* and the lesson 'Push and pull' on page 75 in this book.

## Key background information

As this is a small group activity you may wish to build some time in to the lesson to allow your group to share their findings with the rest of the class.

## Preparation

Set up your 'Pendulum' equipment so that the strings hang down between two tables (see the illustration below). Find a safe place to put the typist's chair. Set out your collection of items nearby. Make copies of photocopiable page 121, one for each child.

## Resources needed

For the introduction it would be helpful to have ready to hand the items used in a previous lesson on pushes and pulls, for example toy cars, balls, doorbell, doll's pram.

For the main part of the lesson you will need a selection of items which demonstrate rocking, spinning or swinging motions. Items might include: home made 'Pendulum' equipment (see the illustration on the previous page) a typist's swivel chair, executive desk-top toys which swing and swivel, clocks with pendulums (including those with a rotating action), a rocking horse, spinning tops (either bought or home-made), a rocking chair. You may be able to make use of your school's large play apparatus or combine this science lesson with a visit to the local park to play on swings and roundabouts. You will also need paper, photocopiable page 121, writing materials.

## Language to be introduced

Rock, spin, swivel, swing, push, pull, start, stop, move, speed up, slow down, change direction, travel.

## What to do

Take the children to the place where you have set out your collection of objects. Explain that they are going to investigate the different ways the various items in your collection move. If you have carried out the previous activity, remind them that they have already looked at the movement of items which can be pushed or pulled. Can they remember what some of these items were?

Look at the collection of objects together and encourage the children to describe the movements which they can see (for example the swinging pendulum in a clock). Next remove any items from the collection which it would be inappropriate for them to handle, for instance any valuable or fragile items, and allow them time to investigate the

different movements. Talk to the children as they investigate, encouraging them to describe the movement which they are seeing and experiencing. When all the children have investigated the items in your collection, bring them together and use the words collected earlier to group the items. *Which items should we put into the group for spinning? Which items rock?* Allow the children to record the groups.

Safety considerations will limit the number of concurrent investigations, depending on the levels of adult supervision you have available. Can the children use words to describe the movements? Record their words for later use.

Give each child a copy of photocopiable page 121. Discuss the different items on the sheet and how they move before asking the children to complete the sentences. They could also draw in arrows to show the direction of movement.

## Suggestion(s) for extension

Try changing the materials hung from the string of the pendulums. You could use lumps of plasticine, conkers or other resilient materials.

## Suggestion(s) for support

To simplify the activity, introduce just one form of movement at a time. You could also have separate lessons looking at things that move like a swing, things that spin like a roundabout, things that rock like a cradle, and so on.

## Display ideas

The pendulums can form part of an interactive display which includes questions and challenges to keep the children investigating. For instance: *Can you make the pendulum move slowly? Can you swing one pendulum to make all the others move?*

## Other aspects of the Science PoS covered

Physical Processes 2a. Experimental and Investigative Science 1a, 1b, 2a, 3a, 3e, 3f. Section 0 1a, 1b, 2a, 3a, 4a, 4b.

## Reference to photocopiable sheet

Photocopiable page 121 requires the children to record the movement of the items drawn on the sheet. The children could also draw lines and arrows to show the direction of movement. You may wish to make one enlarged copy and use it as a class recording sheet.

## SHAKE, RATTLE AND ROLL

*To describe how things move, speed up and change direction.*

✝✝ *Class or group investigation.*

🕐 *30 minutes.*

⚠ *Safety: Stress the importance of not putting dice and tiddlywinks into mouths, noses and ears.*

## Previous skills/knowledge needed

It would be helpful if the children had used the language of forces in different contexts by doing, for example, the activities entitled 'Push and pull' and 'The tube' on pages 75 and 87 in this book or the activities on pages 74–79 in *Curriculum Bank Science, Key Stage One*.

## Preparation

Organize your resources so that each group carrying out the activity can have easy access to them. Make sufficient copies of photocopiable page 122 so that there is one copy for each group. You may also wish to prepare a target for simple maths work. An adapted copy of photocopiable page 122 would suffice.

## Resources needed

If they are available use a bucket and large floor dice. If not, use ordinary dice with a shaker. Each group of six children will need at least 36 tiddlywinks and a variety of pots for the tiddlywinks to be fired into. If you are using a mixture of large and small tiddlywinks then put out a sufficient amount of large ones so that there is one for each child in the group. For the extension activity – a variety of surfaces, for example a carpet tile, cutting board and newspaper. Photocopiable page 122.

## Language to be introduced

Press, flick, travel, bounce, high, higher, lower, force, change direction, up, fall, down, slow, fast, roll, jump.

## What to do

Gather the children into a circle. Shake the dice in a bucket then roll it into the middle of the circle. Ask the children if they can think of words or phrases to describe how the dice moved. Encourage as many children as possible to suggest answers in order to collect a wide variety of words. Suggestions may include 'roll', 'rock', 'over and over', 'change direction', 'go another way' and so on.

Shake the dice again. This time, as you are shaking it, tell the children you want them to be very clever and to think of a word that has not already been suggested to describe how the dice moves. Shake the dice really hard and roll it across the circle. Did the dice move in a different way? Did it move faster/slower/further? Did it go higher into the air? Can the children explain why? Do they know that it is something to do with the force you used to shake and roll the dice?

Talk to the children about the way familiar objects fly through the air. Can they tell you what makes a ball travel faster or slower? Ask them to describe what happens to a ball when it is thrown. Can they describe the trajectory or pathway of the ball?

Tell the children that they are going to investigate some other objects that fly through the air: tiddlywinks. Demonstrate how to make the tiddlywinks fly through the air by flipping one with another. Ask the children to explain why the tiddlywinks do not always travel in the same direction or fly at the same height. Can they use the language of forces to explain their ideas? *Why do the tiddlywinks sometimes fly higher? What would I have to*

*do to make the tiddlywinks go into this pot? Where should I press on this tiddlywink to make it go in this direction?*

Organize the children into pairs within groups of six and allow them to investigate firing the tiddlywinks into a pot for themselves. When they are able to fire their tiddlywinks into their pot, change the pot for a different-sized one or move it to a different place. Is it easier or harder to fire the tiddlywinks into the new pot? What makes it easier or harder? Do the children need to change the way they press the tiddlywink? Do they need to press it in a different place for it to go in a different direction?

At the end of the lesson, draw the children together to discuss their findings. Look at the pots that the children were able to fire their tiddlywinks into. How many tiddlywinks went into pots altogether? Was it easier to fire the large tiddlywinks or the small ones? Are the children able to say what makes a good and bad shot? Did they successfully manage to fire their tiddlywinks into the pot when it was moved to a different place? Encourage them to use the language of forces as they give their explanations, for example using words such as 'press', 'flick', 'push'.

## Suggestion(s) for extension

Older or more able children may wish to investigate the difference made when firing the tiddlywinks from different surfaces. A chart of results can be made by counting the number of successful shots achieved on each surface. By using photocopiable page 122 as a simple target it is possible to extend the activity into a simple maths exercise. Explain to the children that they must try to land their tiddlywinks onto the different numbers on the sheet. You can either ask the children to add their scores from the target or, for more advanced work, keep a tally of the numbers which each tiddlywink lands on to produce a frequency chart.

## Suggestion(s) for support

For those children unlikely to be able to carry out the investigation independently, the level of adult support will need to be carefully considered. Some young children find it difficult to manipulate the tiddlywinks. Providing larger counters such as plastic coins from your maths resources may help these children. Many different plastic objects can be flicked to produce a jump. For example, try pressing on the edge of a unifix cube with your finger or thumb. The resulting 'jump' can be quite spectacular.

## Assessment opportunities

This activity has the potential to identify the most able thinkers. A hard press on a tiddlywink does not always produce a high or long flight. The more advanced thinker should be making a connection between the force being applied and the other variables involved such as the surface, the angle of press, the speed of the flick.

## Opportunities for IT

The number of successful pots and/or tiddlywinks can be recorded onto a frequency chart set up on a simple data handling package. A comparison of the results, for example whether more tiddlywinks landed in large or small pots, can be included.

## Display ideas

Make a large target for the children to use, to develop their tiddlywink playing skills into a mathematics game. This can be placed on a large table top for the children to use as an interactive display.

## Other aspects of the Science PoS covered

Physical Processes 2a. Experimental and Investigative Science 2a, 2b, 2c. Section 0 1a, 3a, 4a, 5a, 5b

## Reference to photocopiable sheet

Photocopiable page 122 is a target which can be enlarged for the children to use for their continuing investigations into the forces needed to propel the tiddlywinks. To use different combinations of numbers, make one copy before deleting and adding your chosen numbers and making enough copies for the group.

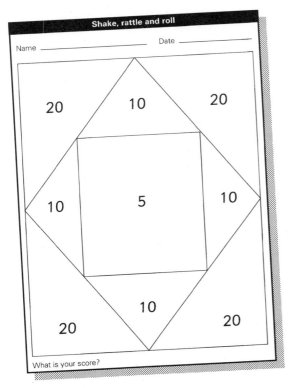

Shake, rattle and roll

Name _____    Date _____

20    10    20

10    5    10

10    20

What is your score?

# FAN THE KIPPER

**To know that moving air is a force which makes things move.**

†† *Class or group activity.*

🕐 *30 minutes*

## Previous skills/knowledge needed

This lesson would link well with 'Run like the wind' on page 85 of this book. These two activities can be carried out in any order.

## Preparation

Arrange to use the hall for this lesson. Ask the children to bring in a glossy colour magazine from home, such as a TV listings magazine. Bring in some magazines yourself for children who do not bring in their own. Make sure there are sufficient pages to provide one page per pupil. Either draw your own kipper shape or use the template on photocopiable page 123 , copying it onto a sheet of glossy newsprint. Depending on how you carry out the activity, you may want to make kipper shapes for all the children (see 'What to do'). The activity in this lesson is inherently safe but is very exciting for the children. If working with the whole class or a large group you will need to organize the activity so that smaller groups of children take turns to fan their 'kippers'.

## Resources

Sufficient glossy colour magazines (at least one per child), scissors, sticky tape, photocopiable page 123.

## Language to be introduced

Push, flap, fan, air, movement, wind, float, glide, rise, fall, twist, turn.

## What to do

Tear out a sheet from a colour magazine and allow it to float to the floor. Discuss with the children the way it moves. Does it fall straight to the ground, or does it fall gently moving from side to side? Can the children explain why it floats?

Now place the sheet of paper on the surface of a table where everyone can see it. Ask a child to blow it along the table but do not allow him or her to touch it. Ask the other children to watch what happens and to describe and explain what they observe. Can anyone suggest a way of making the piece of paper move better/faster? You may like to develop the lesson at this point into an investigation, allowing the children to investigate different ways the paper could be folded to make it a 'good mover'. Listen to the children's ideas and try some of them out. They could either be tried out separately or as races. Make a note of the children's modifications to the piece of paper and try to reach agreement with them over which modifications led to real improvements.

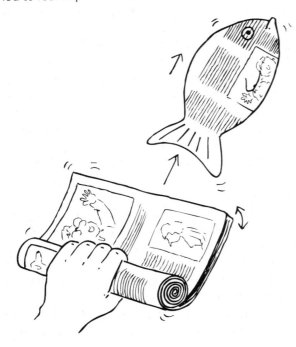

Check that the children understand what is making the paper move. Ask them to explain where they think the wind (or moving air) is pushing on the paper. Now explain that they are going to play a game called 'Fan the kipper'. In this game the wind or moving air is provided by fanning rather than blowing. Using a magazine, vigorously fan the sheet of paper across the table.

Help the children tear out a page from their magazine and show them the 'kipper' which you made earlier. Using this page, ask the children to cut out a 'good' kipper shape; one which they think will be good when fanned, for instance should the kipper be big or small, wide or narrow, bent or flat? Alternatively, you could provide ready-prepared kippers made from the template on photocopiable page 123 or a template of your own design.

Now take the children to the hall and tell them to 'fan their kippers' using a rolled-up magazine. Allow them as much free investigation as possible, noting those who are having significant successes and failures. After an appropriate amount of time, draw all the children together. Ask some of the more successful children to demonstrate their kippers and fanning techniques. Encourage all the children to describe the way in which the kippers move along the hall floor, introducing new language as appropriate. Back in the classroom draw all the language together to form a report of the activity.

**Suggestion(s) for extension**
Some children may be able to explore a range of different papers and make judgements about their suitability as 'kippers'. Older children could carry out fair tests using a range of papers but keeping the kipper size constant. Challenge the more able children to identify as many variables as they can.

## Suggestion(s) for support

Additional adult support will give the children more opportunities to use appropriate language to describe the movement of the paper. Many will also benefit from help with the cutting of the kipper shape and bending it to catch the wind.

## Assessment opportunities

Make a note of those children who include in their explanations the understanding that the air is acting as a supporting/lifting factor. Similarly, note those who connect the force of fanning with the resulting movement of the kipper. If the children have designed their own kipper shape, you will be able to make judgements about their understanding based both on the shape they have made and also from the way in which they tried to move it along.

## Display ideas

Make a display of paintings and pictures of objects which float on air such as paragliders, kites, gliders, feathers, leaves and seeds.

## Other aspects of the Science PoS covered

Experimental and Investigative Science 1a, 1b, 1c, 2a, 2b, 2c, 3a, 3c, 3d, 3f. Section 0 1a, 1b, 3a, 4b.

## Reference to photocopiable sheet

Photocopiable page 123 is a template which can be used to make 'kipper' shapes for the children to fan during the activity.

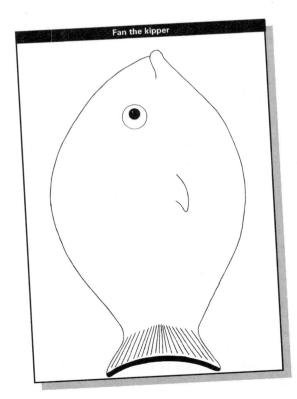

**Fan the kipper**

# FORCES IN A BOTTLE

*Forces make things start, stop and change direction.*

†† *Class introduction followed by group investigation.*

🕐 *30 minutes.*

⚠ *Safety: Stress to the children that the liquid used in this activity is not suitable for drinking.*

## Previous skills/knowledge needed

This activity is based on careful observation. Although it is not essential for children to have had previous experience in describing scientific phenomena, it would be a useful skill for this activity.

## Preparation

Fill a range of plastic bottles with varying amounts of (coloured) water. Have some water ready to add to bottles during the investigation.

## Resources needed

A collection of plastic, transparent drinks bottles with tops. Some bottles in the collection should be identical for fair testing. Ideally, you should provide a pair of identical bottles for each pair of children carrying out the investigation. For the extension activity – a water supply, a jug, funnel and large bowl. For the support activity – a range of different materials, such as rice, sand, salt.

## Language to be introduced

Forwards, backwards, moving, movement, rocking, swaying, slower, faster, roll, rolling, liquid.

## What to do

Show the children an empty plastic bottle and ask them how it will move when it is pushed along the ground. Lay the bottle down on its side and push it along. Give the children time to describe the movement of the bottle. Does it roll or slide? Is it moving forwards or backwards? Ask the children to predict what will happen if you give the bottle a harder push. Pull the bottle towards you. What do the children notice? Elicit from them the fact that pushing and pulling the bottle will make it start to move. Reinforce the use of forces words such as 'push', 'pull' and 'change direction'. Now ask them what will happen if the bottle is part-filled with water and pushed along the ground. Can they predict how the movement might be different from the empty bottle? Part fill a bottle with water and push it along the ground. Again, ask the children to describe the movement of the bottle. Does it move forwards or backwards or both? Write down the words the children suggest for later use in a display.

Organize the children into pairs and tell them that they are going to investigate how two bottles move when

varying amounts of liquid, in this case water, is put inside. Hand out two bottles per pair. If appropriate, ask the children why you are using identical bottles and spend some time discussing fair testing. Explain that you want the children to think of ways to describe how the bottles are moving. Set the children to work rolling the various bottles. Visit the various groups during the activity to listen to the children's conversations and to focus their thinking on the language of forces. How do the children describe the movement of the water? Do they notice that the water stops moving at some point and starts to rock to and fro, thus changing the direction of the movement of the bottle. Encourage the children to describe exactly how the bottle is moving by asking questions such as *Is it rocking? Is it going backwards and forwards?*

Finish the lesson by bringing the class back together and looking at the language brought out in the activity. Explain to the children that when the bottle is rocking it is in fact changing direction. The push makes the bottle move. The movement of the water gradually comes to a stop and starts to move in a different direction. This acts as a force and makes the bottle stop and change direction.

### Suggestion(s) for extension

Some children may wish to investigate what happens to the movement when varying amounts of water are added to the bottles. This can be organized by having a selection of bottles already filled with water or by allowing the children to add water themselves using a jug, funnel and

a bowl. More able children could add pre-specified amounts of water using standard and non standard measures.

### Suggestion(s) for support

Additional adult helpers would contribute greatly to the development of descriptive language. Children who need additional experience to develop the concepts developed by this activity can repeat the lesson using a range of different materials in the bottles, such as sand, rice, salt and so on.

### Assessment opportunities

Note those children who are able to describe the movement of the bottles and also develop an hypothesis to explain the change in movement when liquid is added to the bottle.

### Display ideas

Use the language collected to form a display of movement words.

### Other aspects of the Science PoS covered

Experimental and Investigative Science 1a, 1b, 1c, 2a, 3a, 3c, 3e, 3f. Section 0 4a, 3a.

# RUN LIKE THE WIND

**To know that the forces of pushes and pulls make things speed up, slow down and change direction.**

†† *Whole class activity or group activity.*

🕐 *40 minutes.*

⚠ *Safety: There is potential danger in the running activity part of this lesson. It is strongly recommended that you carry out a risk assessment before attempting the activity.*

## Previous skills/knowledge needed

It would be useful if the children had talked about the movement of objects in the environment on a windy day. For example the difference in movement between the branches swaying on a tree and leaves being blown about.

## Preparation

For obvious reasons you will need to allow time in your weekly planning for this activity to take place on a windy day. Cut some card to an appropriate size so that the children will find it easy to handle, but large enough to feel the force of the wind. Dutch grey board is an ideal material to use as it is not sharp, will bend easily and cushion the fall a little should a child fall over. You will also need a classroom assistant to help you when the children are outside. Make copies of photocopiable page 124, one for each child. Make copies of photocopiable page 125 for those children carrying out the extension activity.

## Resources needed

Some sheets of newspaper (tabloid size) and an equal number of large (about A1 size) sheets of thick card. The actual numbers required will depend both on your class size and your assessment of risk. It is recommended that only half the class move with the boards at any one time. With very young children, you should organize additional adult support so that they can do the practical part of this activity in small groups of no more than six children. Photocopiable page 124. For the extension activity – photocopiable page 125.

## Language to be introduced

Force, push, pull, change direction, blow, blew.

## What to do

Talk about windy days with the children. Ask them to explain what makes things fly about on a windy day. If you can see out of your classroom window, ask the children to explain why some things are moving and other things are staying still. What is pushing the leaves/litter about? Why is the school not lifted up by the wind? Talk about how the branches on the trees sway from side to side but do not move from one place to another. Tell the children that they are going to investigate the force of the wind, the moving air which makes things move.

Talk to the children about what it feels like to be outside on a windy day. Has the wind ever pushed against them so strongly that they felt they were going to be pushed over? Explain that the wind is a force which pushes. The

faster it moves, the more push it has. Does it have a lot of push today?

Make sure the children are dressed appropriately then take them outside so that they can feel the wind. Allow them to run and twirl in the wind for a short time then call them together. Ask them what they could feel when they ran in the wind. Did they find it easy? Be prepared for the inevitable 'yes'. Hold up a sheet of newspaper. What do the children think will happen to it if you let it go? It may already be blowing about. Hold the piece of paper up and ask the children to show you where the wind is pushing. How do they know? Is the paper bending in that place? Now take your large piece of board. Where is the wind pushing on the board? Do the children think that the wind will push with a greater force on the big board than on the smaller piece of paper?

Explain to the children that you want them to run around the playground, first holding the newspaper in front of them and then the board. With the support of a good classroom assistant, divide the children into groups. Hand out the sheets of newspaper and tell them to continue with the practical part of the activity. When they have tested the newspaper, exchange it for the board and repeat the running.

When they have finished, ask them what they noticed. Many will already be so excited about feeling the pushing force of the wind that they will already be telling you about the force they felt. Some small children will find this activity almost impossible on a windy day, as they may not be strong enough to hold onto the board and will find it very hard to battle against the force. They should notice that the wind almost makes them stop.

When all the children have investigated using both materials, return to the classroom and talk about the difference felt between holding the newspaper and the board. Explain that the wind is a pushing force which makes things move, but which also makes things stop. Hand out copies of photocopiable page 124 and ask the children to complete it.

### Suggestion(s) for extension

Introduce the Beaufort wind scale. Hand out copies of photocopiable page 125. Explain to the children that they can use this to judge the force of the wind on the day of the activity with subsequent days. They should draw in pictures of the things that they observed being moved about by the wind and then note down which was the windiest day.

### Suggestion(s) for support

Some children who have mobility difficulties may find this activity too difficult to do unaided. Additional safety considerations will have to be taken. On a windy day, it may be enough for them to hold the newspaper and board in front of them and feel the force.

### Assessment opportunities

Ask the children to use the word 'Push' in a sentence to describe what the wind does. More able children may be able to explain the relationship between the varying force of the wind and the varying force of trees, litter and so on.

### Display ideas

This activity links well with the story *The Wind Blew* by Pat Hutchings (Red Fox). You could use the children's experience and the ideas in the book to mount a display showing what the force of the wind can do. *Mrs Mopples Washing Line* by Anita Hewett is another favourite story.

### Other aspects of the Science PoS covered

Experimental and Investigative Science 1a, 1b, 1c, 2a, 2b, 3a, 3b, 3c, 3d, 3e, 3f. Section 0 1a, 1b, 2a, 3a, 4a, 5b.

### Reference to photocopiable sheets

Photocopiable page 124 provides the opportunity for the children to demonstrate their understanding of forces. Photocopiable page 125 is a recording sheet for the children to keep a diary of the movement of things in the environment caused by the wind.

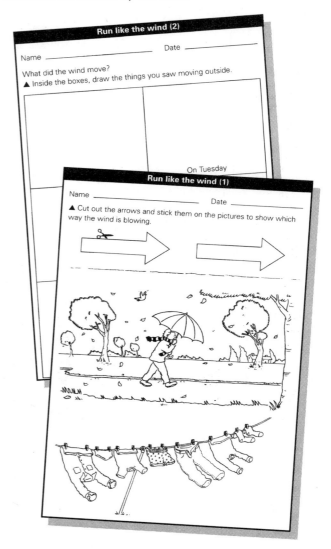

**THE TUBE**

*Some objects made from certain materials can have their shape changed by squashing, bending and twisting. Forces can change the shape of objects.*

†† *Class introduction activity followed by group investigation.*

🕐 *40 minutes.*

⚠ *Safety: When carrying out the group investigation using the tray and cardboard tubes, be very careful that the children keep their distance and are not in danger of catching their fingers. It is best to carry out the group investigation on a carpeted area on the floor so that falling weights and objects do not crush toes. Also check your LEA safety policy if you are thinking of using toilet rolls for this activity.*

## Previous skills/knowledge needed

A good introduction to this lesson would be to look at the use of tubes in and around your school. You may find tubes in construction toys, in the fabric of the building or classroom furniture. Look for pipes carrying services. It would be helpful if the children had previously considered why tubes are used so frequently in our environment.

## Key background information

Some children may relate the human use of tubes to plants and stems. If this is raised then a study of dandelion stems might follow.

## Preparation

Collect or make some cardboard tubes. The tubes inside kitchen rolls are suitable but please see the note above on the use of toilet rolls. At least some of the tubes should be of a consistent size. Place the tubes on a table with a child's drawer tray balanced on top. Try using five tubes of equal size: one in each corner and one supporting the centre of the tray.

Have some heavy objects ready to hand. You can use 1kg masses or any objects that the children recognize as being 'heavy'. If your group numbers are fairly large you will also need to organize plenty of adult support for the second part of the lesson in which the children carry out their own investigations. Make copies of photocopiable page 126, one for each child.

## Resources needed

A collection of cardboard tubes, a sufficient amount of rolled paper tubes for every child in the group to have at least two. A child's drawer tray. Heavy objects and/or masses. An empty crushed drinks can. Photocopiable page 126.

## Language to be introduced

Squash, buckle, bend, twist, strain, crush, crumple, tear, stress, tube, roll, pipe.

## What to do

Gather the children together and remind them of the work they did looking for tubes around the school. Ask them if they can remember where they saw some tubes or tube shapes. Can they remember how they were used? Remind them of drainpipes, lampposts, telegraph poles, chair and table legs, television aerials and so on. Explain that one of the reasons why tubes are often used is because it is a strong shape which is not easily squashed or broken. Explain to the children that they are going to look at the way tubes can have their shape altered by squashing,

twisting or bending. Give one child a rolled paper tube. Ask if the children think it is very strong. Encourage them to give reasons for their answers. Then encourage the child with the tube to bend, squash or twist it.

Look at the tube together and observe what has happened to it. Were the children right? Has the tube been ripped? Has it been squashed, crushed, crumpled? Continue to extend the children's use of language until they are able to describe what has happened to the tube. Now take a cardboard tube and ask the children to predict how easy it would be to change the shape of this tube. Again, encourage the children to give reasons for their predictions. Give another child the opportunity to try to change the shape of the tube by bending, squashing or twisting it. Look carefully at what has happened. Put the paper tube and the cardboard tube side by side so that the children can see both tubes clearly. Explain that the shape of both tubes has been changed because of the forces (pushes, pulls and twists) inflicted upon them by the children. Discuss with the children where the weak spots of the tubes are. Are they at the ends or in the middle of the tubes? What do you have to do to change the shape of the tube? Most children will probably say that you have to twist the tube in order to break or alter it. Some may describe how they could increase the force, for example by stamping on the tube. Draw out as many science related teaching points as you feel appropriate from the ensuing discussion. Do the children still think that a tube is a strong shape?

Now turn to the tray which you have previously set up on the table. Ask the children to predict what they are going to watch. They may think that they have proved that the tube is not a strong shape. You are about to prove otherwise by adding more and more weight to the tray. The tray will take an enormous amount of weight. The exact amount will depend on the tubes and the balance of

the tray. It is possible to support the weight of one or two heavy adults using five cardboard tubes! However, it is not recommended that you try to emulate this awesome feat! Explain that the weight is a pushing force which is trying to squash the tubes.

Now allow all the children the opportunity to investigate some paper tubes and cardboard tubes. This can be a little chaotic and very noisy if carried out on tables so it is best to ensure that all the children are working on a mat or carpeted area of the floor. You will also need additional adult support for this part of the lesson if your group numbers are large. If you have a classroom assistant, give him or her prompt sheets to develop the children's understanding that tubes can have their shapes changed by twisting and squashing. However, stress that tubes are still strong as their shapes are able to carry a lot of weight when standing on their end. Tubes are easier to squash, crush and twist in some places than others: they have weak spots. Help the children to record what they have seen and understood. Hand out copies of photocopiable page 126. Point to the picture of the tube and explain that you want the children to colour in the strongest and weakest places. They can then complete the sentence at the bottom of the page by writing in what force they used to change the shape of the tube.

## Suggestion(s) for extension
After carrying out the assessment activity opposite, use empty drinks cans to investigate the effects of crushing. Look for 'crumpled' areas. Relate the crushed cans to the use of 'crumple zones' in cars.

## Suggestion(s) for support
Use a collection of tubes to increase the children's practical experience. Include tubes from sweets, pipes, kitchen rolls and so on and encourage the children to add to the

collection. Sort the collection for different attributes. One of the sorting exercises could be used as an assessment opportunity for this lesson, for instance sorting for strength.

## Assessment opportunities

Show the children a crushed drinks can and try to identify those children who are able to say what has happened to the can. Are they able to explain that the shape of the can has been changed by squashing or crushing. Which children are able to point to the spot or area where the force was applied?

## Display ideas

Use the collection of crushed tubes (and cans if used) to form a backdrop to the display of language you wish to develop. Create a tubes collection and add appropriate questions to encourage the children to sort and re-sort the collection.

## Other aspects of the Science PoS covered

Physical processes 2d. Experimental and Investigative Science 3c. Section 0 1a, 2a, 4a.

## Reference to photocopiable sheet

Photocopiable page 126 is a recording sheet for the children to label the weakest and strongest parts of the tube. The sentence at the bottom should be completed with the word or words which describe the force needed to change the shape of the tube.

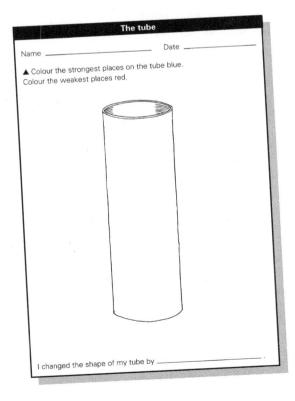

The tube

Name _____ Date _____

▲ Colour the strongest places on the tube blue.
Colour the weakest places red.

I changed the shape of my tube by _____

# PLAYING IN THE DARK

*We need light in order to see things.*

†† *Whole class introduction followed by group activity.*

🕑 *45 minutes.*

⚠ *Safety: Choose your materials with safety in mind. Black bin liners can be good for blocking out light but it is suggested that you cut them up so that children are not tempted to pull them over their heads. Also, use string and tape rather than pins. Staples can be used safely with a little extra care. Drawing pins are best avoided as they are easily pulled out and can be stepped or knelt on by the children who will not see them in the dark.*

## Previous skills/knowledge needed

Prior to this activity take, or arrange for the children to be taken, around the school in small groups to find a dark place.

## Preparation

The activity needs an area in or just outside the classroom where it is easy for the children to drape or attach a variety of materials and fabrics to stable objects. Clothes airers are often a good starting point and are large enough for the children to enter afterwards. If possible the area should contain little natural light. Try out a range of fasteners and tapes to find the best one to use to attach the fabrics and materials without permanently damaging the walls and fixtures. Staples and carpet tape have been found to be the strongest and cause the least damage. Make copies of photocopiable page 127, one for each child. Make copies of photocopiable page 128 for less able children.

## Resources needed

A variety of dark materials and fabrics such as unwanted sheets, blankets, opaque plastic sheets, curtains, offcuts in a variety of thicknesses; gunstapler and staples, carpet tape, sticky tape, clothes pegs, clothes airer. An area for constructing the dark place. Photocopiable pages 127 and 128.

## Language to be introduced

Dark, darker, darkest, darkness, light, bright, blocking out, absence, day, night, thick, thin.

## What to do

After the children have investigated dark areas around the school, talk to them about the places they found. Who found a dark place? What made it a dark place? How could they make it darker? Which was the darkest place? Why was this the darkest place? Explain that the reason why this place was dark was because it blocked out the most light. Darkness is the absence of light. Talk to the children

about what happens when there is no light. Some will tell you that they cannot see very well and that it is hard to find things in the dark. It may be appropriate to explain at this point that light is needed in order to be able to see.

Tell the children that they are going to make a dark place in the classroom. Show the children the fabrics and other materials you have collected. Choose a fairly thin material and hold it up for the children to see. Allow them to feel it and try to see through it. Ask them whether the material is thick or thin. Do they think this fabric would be good for making a dark place. Would it be good for blocking out the light? Encourage the children to explain why it would or would not make a good light blocker and thus make a good dark place. Stress to the children that the material which blocks out the most light is the best material with which to make a dark place. Continue to hold up different materials and fabrics and discuss whether they would make good light blockers.

Divide the class into groups of four or six. Show the children your selection of materials and set them to work to make their dark place. (Alternatively, you may prefer a small group to work with an additional adult helper while other activities are going on.) When the place or places are finished, allow all the children to go inside to test whether the place is really dark. This will create a great deal of excitement if the activity has been successful.

Gather the class together to discuss what they have done. How did they create their dark place? Why did they choose the materials they did? Were they successful? Is their place the darkest they can make or do they think

they could make one darker? How? Reinforce the learning objective at this point. Distribute copies of photocopiable page 127. Spaces are provided on the sheet for the children to record the good and not so good light blockers. Less able children may benefit from using photocopiable page 128. This has illustrations of various materials. The children are required to put a tick or a cross against each picture depending on whether they think it is an effective light blocker or not.

## Suggestion(s) for extension

The dark place can be used to develop other concepts of darkness and light, for example that light is essential for seeing things; that shiny things need light for them to be seen as they are reflective. Some children can use their knowledge and understanding of electricity to create a circuit so that they can see in their dark place.

## Suggestion(s) for support

Play a game of find the thimble in the classroom and in your dark place. The children will find it easier to find the thimble in the light than in the dark. This will reinforce the concept that we need light to see and that darkness is the absence of light, therefore we cannot see objects in the dark.

## Assessment opportunities

Make a note of the children who are able to explain that:
▲ darkness is the absence of light;
▲ we need light to see things.

## Display ideas

Make a collection of light sources and display these next to your dark place. This should include a picture or model of the sun. There are also a number of appropriate stories which you could read to the children to reinforce the concept, such as *Can't you sleep little bear?* by Martin Waddell (Walker Books).

## Other aspects of the Science PoS covered

Experimental and Investigative Science 2a. Section 0 1a, 3a.

## Reference to photocopiable sheets

Photocopiable page 127 is a sheet on to which the children can record good and not so good light blockers. Photocopiable page 128 is for very young or less able children. The children have to tick or cross each picture depending on whether or not it is a good light blocker.

# THE DRAGON'S TREASURE

*There are many kinds of sound and we hear them when they enter the ear.*

†† *Class activity.*

🕐 *30 minutes.*

## Previous skills/knowledge needed

No previous skills or knowledge are essential but this activity builds well on body sound and instrumental work carried out in music lessons.

## Preparation

Organize this lesson so that it takes place in a room where there is plenty of room for the children to sit in a circle. Provide a precious object for the child who is to be 'the dragon' to look after, for instance a favourite toy from the classroom, some keys, a sweet.

## Resources needed

A blindfold, a range of sound makers (this is optional as you can use the children's own vocal or body sounds), a precious object.

## Language to be introduced

Sound, hear, ear, enter (go into) the ear, source of the sound. You may also want to reinforce the language developed in music lessons by asking the children to name the instrument from which the sound is coming.

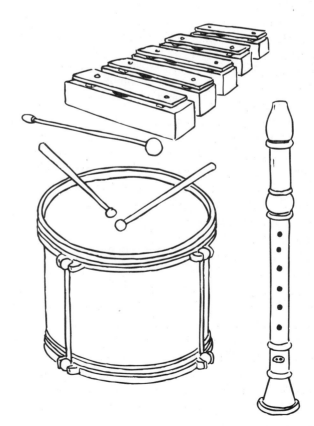

## What to do

Sit the children in a circle and select one child to be 'the dragon'. Show everyone the precious object and explain that you are going to play a listening game. Blindfold the chosen child and ask him or her to sit in the middle of the circle to act as 'dragon'. Place the precious object near the dragon. Choose a different child at random from the circle. Explain that this child is going to try to take the 'treasure' (the precious object) while making a sound. The only way that the precious object can be saved is for the 'dragon' to use its hearing and point straight at the child making the sound.

At this point in the game everyone needs to be very quiet as the 'dragon' needs to be able to pin-point the direction of the sound. Give the second child a percussion instrument and tell him or her to play one note quietly. If the dragon immediately points to the source of the sound then the treasure is safe. Change the child making the sound and the instrument or sound-maker every time. Change the dragon every few turns or after he or she has failed to point at the source of the sound.

At the end of the game talk to the children about how they were able to say where the sound came from. Reinforce the concept that sound travels away from a source, in this case the second child, and can be heard when it enters our ears, in this case the 'dragon'.

## Suggestion(s) for extension

To make the game more difficult, ask the dragon to name the musical instrument being played. The instruments do not have to be played in a 'traditional' manner. Strings can be scraped, drums brushed, chime bars tapped with a finger, and so on.

## Suggestion(s) for support

The game played in this activity can be simplified by being played in small groups. Try playing in groups of five so that the dragon has to point at one of the four corners to identify the source of the sound. If the children need more practice at this activity you could also play the traditional games 'Squeak piggy squeak' or 'Keeper of the keys'.

## Display ideas

Put out a collection of sound sources and a blindfold for the children to use during the week. These can be displayed in front of paintings and drawings the children have made of sound sources.

## Other aspects of the Science PoS covered

Experimental and Investigative Science 1c, 2a. Section 0 3a.

# Shoes

Name _____ Date _____

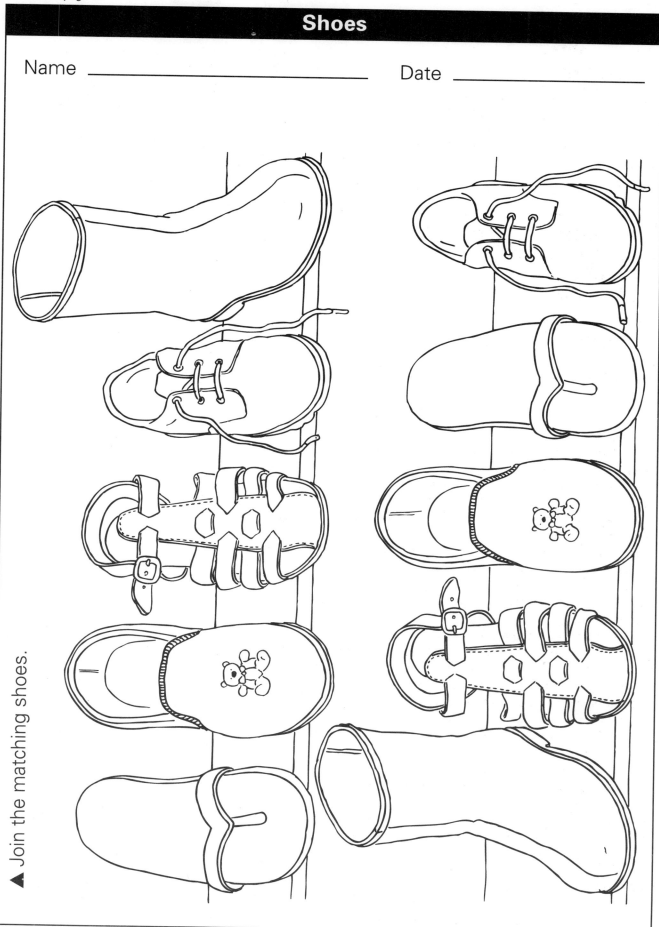

▲ Join the matching shoes.

Squidgy feelings!, see page 14

# Squidgy feelings (1)

Name _____    Date _____

I coloured the bits with little feeling _____.

I coloured the bits with lots of feeling _____.

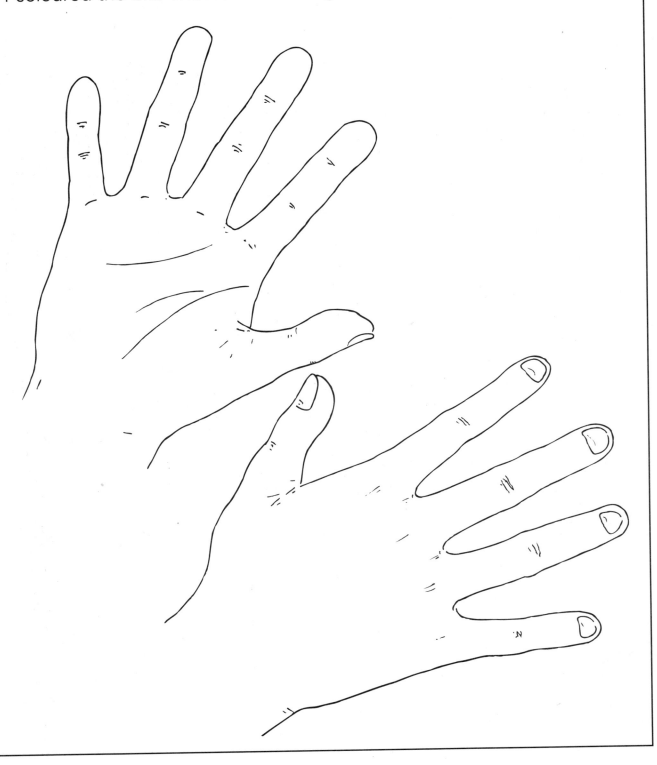

Squidgy feelings!, see page 14

# Squidgy feelings (2)

Name _____    Date _____

I coloured the least tickly bits _____.

I coloured the most tickly bits _____.

Tickling toes, see page 16

# Flooring (1)

Name _____     Date _____

▲ Stick your pieces of flooring inside the squares. Find two words to describe each piece of flooring. Write the words next to the samples.

Stick your piece of
flooring here.

_____

_____

Stick your piece of
flooring here.

_____

_____

Stick your piece of
flooring here.

_____

_____

Tickling toes, see page 16

## Flooring (2)

Name _____    Date _____

▲ Use these words to help you describe the flooring samples.

| 1. | hairy | 7. | warm |
|---|---|---|---|
| 2. | prickly | 8. | cold |
| 3. | fluffy | 9. | soft |
| 4. | bristly | 10. | hard |
| 5. | tickly | 11. | smooth |
| 6. | squashy | 12. | rough |

SCIENCE KEY STAGE ONE

Match my sound, see page 18

## Soundpots

Name _____     Date _____

▲ Colour the stickers to match the sounds you hear.

matches
with

matches
with

matches
with

matches
with

# Identifying Archie

Name _____  Date _____

▲ Record the blemishes and colours of Archie.

▲ Now record the
blemishes and colours
of the apple you chose.

▲ Draw a △ around the things that are the same.

Draw a ◯ around the things that are different.

Coloured milk, see page 24

# Coloured milk (1)

Name _____     Date _____

▲ Which milk will taste the best?

| | | |
|---|---|---|
| Pink | | |
| Green | | |
| Blue | | |
| Yellow | | |
| All the same | | |

This is what we thought after tasting.

| | | |
|---|---|---|
| Pink | | |
| Green | | |
| Blue | | |
| Yellow | | |
| All the same | | |

SCIENCE KEY STAGE ONE

## Coloured milk (2)

Name _____     Date _____

I think this milk will taste the best.

I found out that _____

_____

_____

# Who am I? (1)

Name _____     Date _____

▲ Draw three things that are the same.
Draw three things that are different.

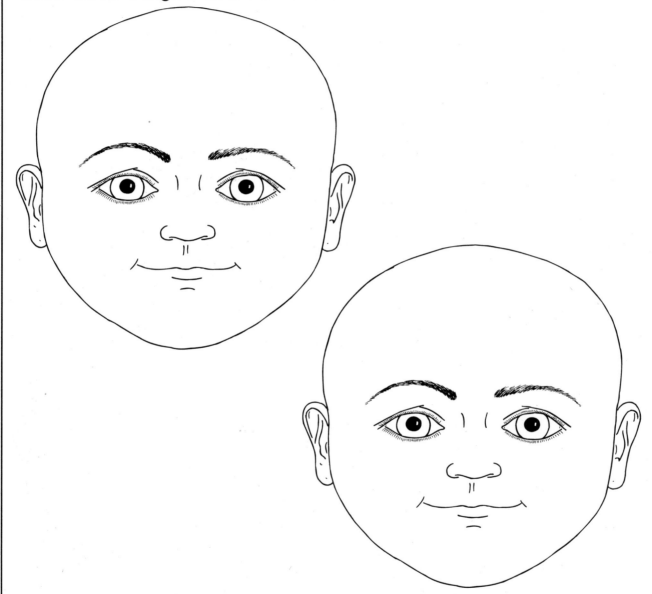

▲ Complete this sentence.

Both faces have _____

but they have different _____

# Who am I? (2)

Name _____  Date _____

▲ Draw in two faces. Make them a bit different from each other.
Now pass the sheet to a friend. Can your friend spot the differences?

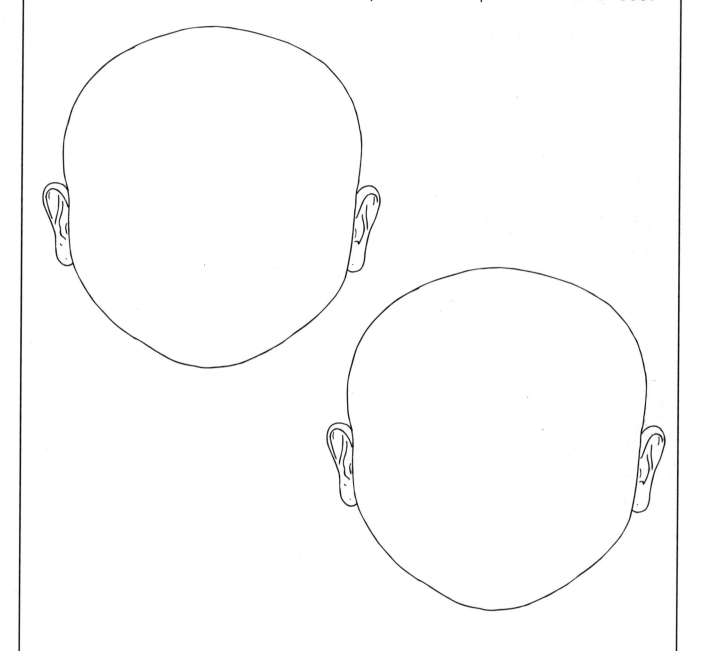

▲ Draw a ⬭ around the things that are different.

Are these my hands?, see page 28

# Block graph

Name _____     Date _____

Title

| | | | |
|---|---|---|---|
| **10** | | | |
| **9** | | | |
| **8** | | | |
| **7** | | | |
| **6** | | | |
| **5** | | | |
| **4** | | | |
| **3** | | | |
| **2** | | | |
| **1** | | | |

**Number of hands**

Leaves, see page 31

# Leaves

Name _____     Date _____

Pumpkins, see page 35

# Pumpkins

Name _____  Date _____

▲ Draw your plantlets. Do they look the same?

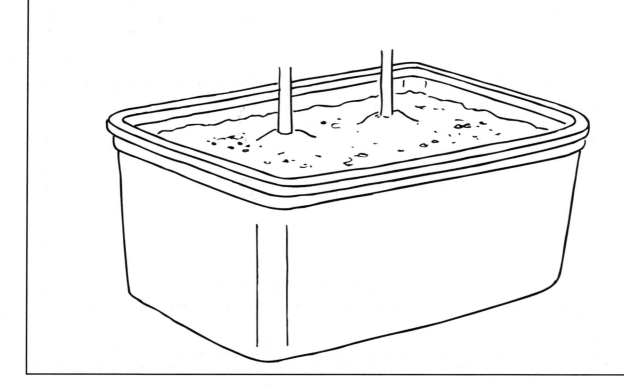

One potato, two potatoes, see page 37

## One potato, two potatoes

Name _____    Date _____

We put the potatoes

|  |  |
|---|---|
| in a wet place. | in a light place. |

It went _____    It went _____

|  |  |
|---|---|
| in a warm place. | in a frosty place. |

It went _____    It went _____

|  |
|---|
| in a dark, dry, cool, frost-free place. |

It _____

# Minibeast safari

Name _____  Date _____

▲ Draw the minibeasts that you found in these different places.

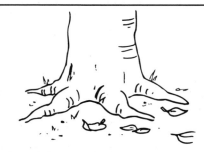

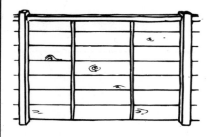

Birds, see page 42

## Birds in the playground

Name _____   Date _____

▲ Record the birds that you see on each day.

| | |
|---|---|
| Monday | |
| Tuesday | |
| Wednesday | |
| Thursday | |
| Friday | |

Wriggling worms, see page 44

# Wriggling worms

Name _____     Date _____

▲ Which food did the worms eat first?

| | | |
|---|---|---|
| | | |

1st                    2nd                    3rd

The worms did not eat

| |
|---|
| |

# A plastic world

Name _____    Date _____

▲ Draw your object in this space.

▲ Now complete this sentence.

The _____ is made from plastic.

It is _____, _____ and

_____.

It is used for _____.

Don't burst my bubble!, see page 57

# Don't burst my bubble!

Name _____     Date _____

▲ Give your bubble blowers marks out of ten.

Tie yourself in knots, see page 59

# Tie yourself in knots

Name _____     Date _____

Gloves to keep you warm, see page 61

# Gloves to keep you warm

Name _____     Date _____

| Material | Will the glove keep my hand warm? | Did the glove keep my hand warm? |
|---|---|---|
| Rubber | | |
| Paper | | |
| Card | | |
| Wool | | |
| Man-made fibre | | |

Bend your image, see page 64

## Mirrors

Name _____  Date _____

▲ Draw and write about your image.

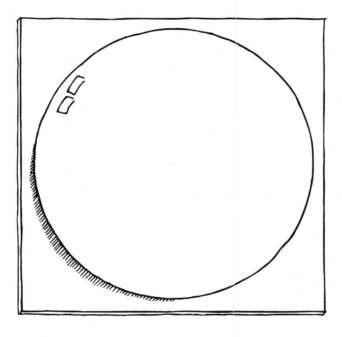

My image is _____

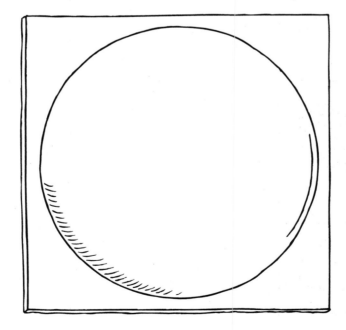

My image is _____

# Burnt toast and hard cheese (1)

Name _____     Date _____

## After

What colour is it now?

◀ Write how it has changed. _____

_____

## Before

What colour is the bread?

◀ Write some words to describe the bread. _____

_____

# Burnt toast and hard cheese (2)

Name _____     Date _____

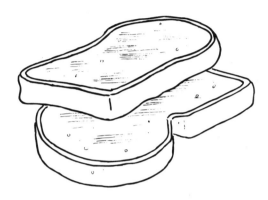

The bread has been toasted.
It has changed colour.

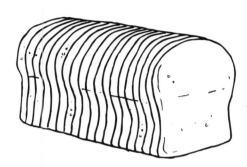

The bread is frozen. It is hard.

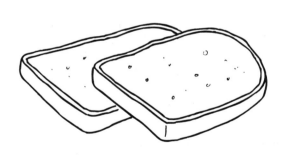

The bread is soft.
It has defrosted.

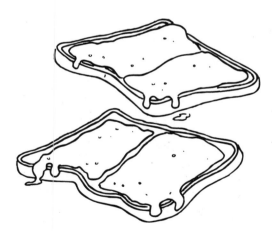

The cheese has melted.
It is soft.

▲ Cut out the pictures and stick them in the right order.

Batteries must be included, see page 73

# Batteries must be included

Name _____    Date _____

Will this bulb light?
▲ Write yes or no
  in the box.

Will this bulb light?
▲ Write yes or no
  in the box.

▲ Draw a ring around the break in the circuit.

Push and pull, see page 75

# Push, pull or push and pull

Name _____ Date _____

These things need a push to start moving.

These things need a pull to start moving.

These things need a push or a pull to start moving.

Push and pull, see page 75

## Push and pull

Name _____    Date _____

▲ Do you push or pull these objects? Write your answers in the boxes.

to write your name

to sit on a chair

to open the door

to kick the football

to turn on the light

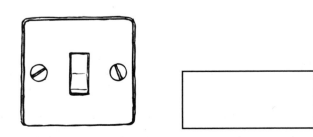

Rock, swivel, spin and swing, see page 77

# Rock, spin and swing

Name _____     Date _____

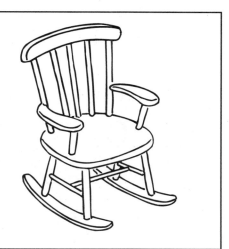

These things _____

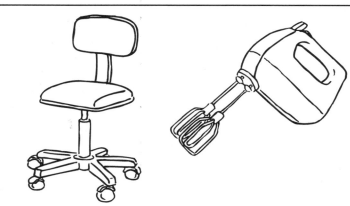

These things _____

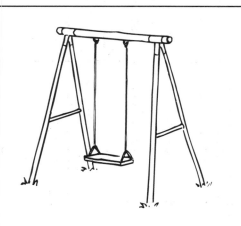

These things _____

▲ Use these words: spin, swing, rock.

# Shake, rattle and roll

Name _____    Date _____

20          10          20

10          5           10

10

20          20

What is your score?

Fan the kipper, see page 81

# Fan the kipper

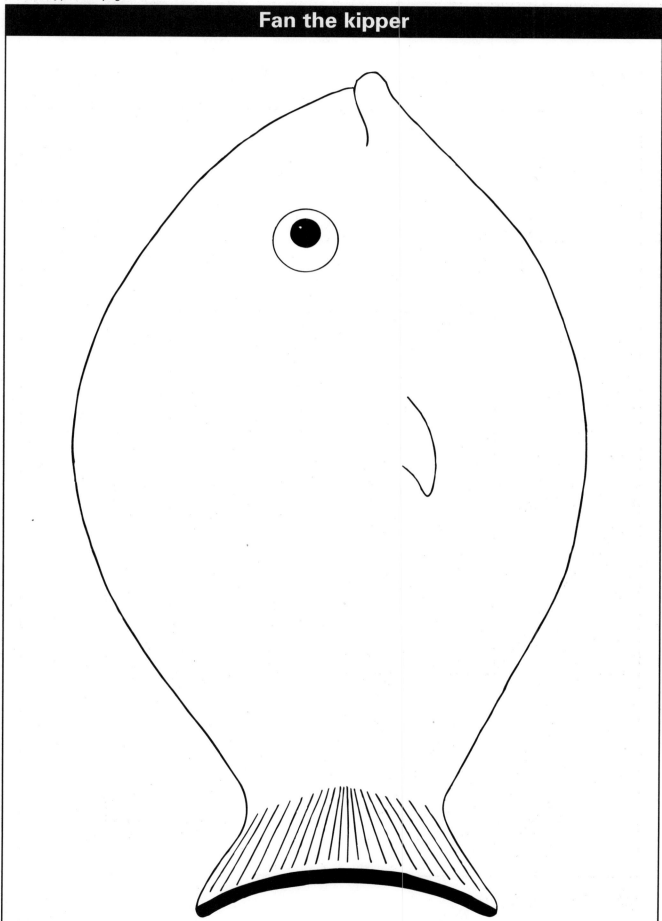

# Run like the wind (1)

Name _____    Date _____

▲ Cut out the arrows and stick them on the pictures to show which way the wind is blowing.

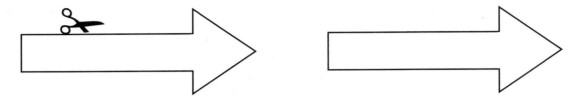

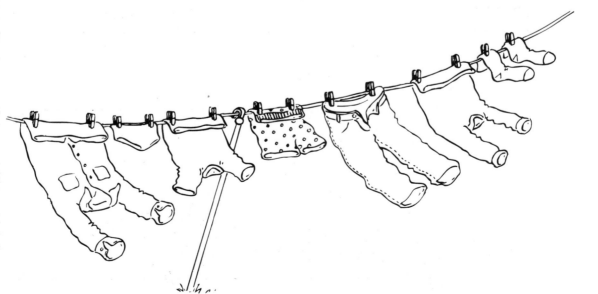

SCIENCE KEY STAGE ONE

# Run like the wind (2)

Name _____     Date _____

What did the wind move?

▲ Inside the boxes, draw the things you saw moving outside.

|  |  |
|---|---|
| On Monday | On Tuesday |
| On Wednesday | On Thursday |
| On Friday | _____<br><br>was the<br><br>windiest day. |

# The tube

Name _____     Date _____

▲ Colour the strongest places on the tube blue.
Colour the weakest places red.

I changed the shape of my tube by _____ .

Playing in the dark, see page 89

# Playing in the dark (1)

Name _____   Date _____

These things are good light blockers.

These things are not good light blockers.

## Playing in the dark (2)

Name _____    Date _____

 Tick the things that are good light blockers.

 Put a cross against the things that are not good light blockers.

glass window

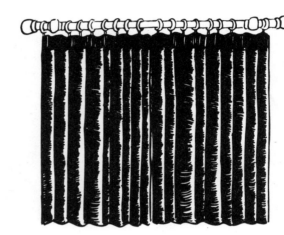

dark curtains

net curtain

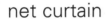

black bin bag

blanket

newspaper